HEALING THEN
AND NOW

Also available in the Pioneer *Perspectives* series:

For further information on the Pioneer *Perspectives* series and Pioneer, please write to:

P.O. Box 79c, Esher, Surrey, KT10 9LP

HEALING THEN AND NOW
Martin Scott

WORD

BOOKS

WORD PUBLISHING
Nelson Word Ltd
Milton Keynes, England

WORD AUSTRALIA
Kilsyth, Victoria, Australia

WORD COMMUNICATIONS LTD
Vancouver, B.C., Canada

STRUIK CHRISTIAN BOOKS (PTY) LTD
Cape Town, South Africa

CHRISTIAN MARKETING NEW ZEALAND LTD
Havelock North, New Zealand

JENSCO LTD
Hong Kong

JOINT DISTRIBUTORS SINGAPORE—
ALBY COMMERCIAL ENTERPRISES PTE LTD
and
CAMPUS CRUSADE, ASIA LTD

SALVATION BOOK CENTRE
Malaysia

HEALING THEN AND NOW

ISBN 0-85009-733-9   (Australia ISBN 1-86258-310-2)

Unless otherwise indicated, Scripture quotations are from the HOLY BIBLE, NEW INTERNATIONAL VERSION (NIV), copyright © 1973, 1978, 1984 by International Bible Society.
Other quotations are from the King James Version of the Bible (KJV).

Front cover illustration: *Waterlilies: Green Reflections*, Monet, courtesy of Musée de l'Orangerie, Paris. Lauros–Giraudon/Bridgeman Art Library (detail).

Reproduced, printed and bound in Great Britain for Nelson Word Ltd. by Cox & Wyman Ltd., Reading.

93 94 95 96 / 10 9 8 7 6 5 4 3 2 1

FOREWORD

Pioneer *Perspectives* are perhaps more than their title suggests!

They are carefully researched presentations of material, on important issues, appealing to thinking churches, creative leaders and responsible Christians.

Each *Perspective* pioneers in as much as it is at the cutting edge of biblical and theological issues. Each will continue to pioneer with new ideas, concepts and data drawn from Scripture, history and a contemporary understanding of both.

They are perspectives in as much as they aim to be an important contribution to the ongoing debate on issues such as women in ministry and leadership; prophets and prophecy in the church; biblical models of evangelism; integrating and discipling new believers; growing and building local churches and further perspectives on Christ's second coming.

Importantly, these studies use a journal style of presentation, and are written by people who are currently working out the implications of the issues they are writing about, in local churches. This is vital if we are to escape the dangerous fantasy of abstract theology without practical experience. They are not written to contribute to the paralysis of analysis—rather to feed, strengthen, nurture and inform so that we can be equipped to get God's will done, by networking the nations with the gospel using all the resources that are available to us.

God's Word is always an event. How much we thank Him that He has left us an orderly account of what He wants us to believe, how He wants us to live, and what He wants us to do in order to bring heaven to the earth. As we embrace a better understanding of Scripture, rooted in local church, national and international mission, we shall become a part of the great eschatological purpose of bringing back the King—not for a church defeated, cowering and retiring but for one which, despite colossal odds, pressures and persecutions, is faithful to her Lord and His Word. To do that we must 'search the Scriptures' to see if many of these 'new things' are true. I commend these *Perspectives* to you as they are published on a regular basis throughout these coming years.

Gerald Coates
Director Pioneer Trust/Team Leader

Pioneer consists of a team and network of churches, committed to dynamic and effective biblical Christianity.

The national team act as advisers and consultants to churches, which in many cases develop into a partnership with the Pioneer team. These are the churches keen to identify with the theology, philosophy, ethos and purpose of Pioneer. The team have a vigorous youth ministry, church-planting strategy and evangelistic emphasis.

Training courses include Equipped to Lead, Emerging Leaders and the highly successful TIE teams (Training In Evangelism).

Pioneer have also been instrumental in initiating and funding March for Jesus (with Ichthus/YWAM); Jubilee Campaign (for the suffering church worldwide); and ACET (Aids Care Education Training).

ACKNOWLEDGEMENTS

There are many people who have influenced my life, my understanding of God and His desire to heal. I want to freely acknowledge the debt I owe to the church community of which I am a part, as it has played a major role in bringing healing to various aspects of my life.

Specifically I am most grateful to my wife, Sue, who has been with me in my journey towards discovering the reality of God's healing power for others.

I could mention many others, but I need specifically to acknowledge two people with healing ministries who have influenced me more than any others in the area of healing. Firstly, Ian Andrews whom I first met in 1984. He left me with a deep desire to see God's power released and was a great encouragement to me in the years that followed. The second person is Michael Kolisang. I have had the privilege of working with him both in his home country of Lesotho and in the UK. His infectious faith and passion for the gospel has stirred me many times to persevere and not grow weary.

I owe a great debt to the many men and women I have never met but who have written on the subject of healing. Of them all, there is one book which I have recommended more than any other in recent years. It is *The Authority to Heal* by Ken Blue (Monarch Publications, 1989). If my short book is able to answer questions and to stir faith to the level achieved by his book, then I will be satisfied.

With regard to the editing of this volume, I want to thank Christine Williamson for her comments which have helped to make this book considerably more readable than the original draft!

Finally, I would like to dedicate this book to Edith, Lucy, Hilary and Charles; and beyond that to all who have experienced miracles in their own bodies; and to those who are yet waiting for God to intervene.

Martin Scott
July 1993

CONTENTS

INTRODUCTION   13

CHAPTER 1:   A Supernatural Church   15

CHAPTER 2:   A Biblical Framework   27

CHAPTER 3:   Pastoral Perspectives   41

CHAPTER 4:   Praying for People who are Sick   49

CHAPTER 5:   Healing and Wholeness   57

CHAPTER 6:   Releasing the Supernatural   71

CHAPTER 7:   The Holy Spirit and Healing   81

APPENDIX 1:   New Testament Exceptions   87

APPENDIX 2:   I'm Not Healed—What Now?   93

APPENDIX 3:   Recommended Reading   96

INTRODUCTION

The subjects of healing and wholeness have appeared on centre stage in recent years. Stories surrounding the lives of such people as Smith Wigglesworth or Kathryn Kuhlman are no longer read only by those who would call themselves Pentecostal. John Wimber has not only been used by God to bring healing to many people, but has also enabled many Christians who would view themselves as quite ordinary to step out and see God bring healing to others through their own prayers.

Healing is on the agenda for many Christians because there is a renewed emphasis from the Holy Spirit. It must remain on the agenda for us, particularly as occult and semi-occult practices increase in popularity. The supernatural ground must not be abandoned and left for New Age theorists to occupy. It is vital for us to be able to give an apologetic which will counteract New Age philosophy, but it is also vital for the church to rise to the challenge and present an alternative to all counterfeit philosophies and practices.

I have been involved in praying for the sick for a number of years. Over that period of time I have seen many wonderful testimonies of healing. I am also honest in saying that in the same period of time there have been some great disappointments, when prayers have not resulted in physical healing. I took a long time to decide to write on the subject of healing, as there is so much good material around—much of it written by those who know more than I do on the matter. However, I have eventually decided to put pen to paper because I believe it is an area where God wants His church to continue to learn. If, through this book, the Lord encourages some to seek Him in order to see a release of the supernatural, then I will feel that this book has served its purpose.

Our theology of healing will certainly influence how we pray, and what we expect God to do for us and through us. However, I am convinced that it will take more than good theology to see God move in healing. Bad theology might well become a hindrance, but correct theology in itself will not be sufficient to release healing. For this reason I do not intend this book to offer principally a theology of healing. Theology will be covered, but I hope it will also be a practical book which will seek to answer some of the difficult questions which surround the subject of healing.

CHAPTER 1

A SUPERNATURAL CHURCH

Jesus promised to build the church, and I for one am very optimistic about the future of His church. I believe in the triumph of the gospel, not in the sense of 'christianising' the nations, but in the sense of impacting the nations and communicating Jesus effectively through both proclamation and demonstration. Luke clearly saw the mission of the early church as being simply the continuation of the mission that Jesus had initiated. He states that his Gospel only recorded the beginnings of Jesus' actions and words (Acts 1:1). By clear implication his second book, the Acts of the Apostles, was to be read as a record of all that Jesus was continuing to do and to teach. For Luke, his second book was really the Acts (and words) of Jesus. From Luke's perspective the church was here to continue the ministry of Jesus.

The church is the main instrument of the kingdom of God in the earth. It is here to proclaim and demonstrate the same kingdom which Jesus declared was at hand (Mark 1:15). Jesus gave a mandate to His disciples to proclaim and demonstrate the kingly rule of God (for example see Luke 10:9). Their proclamation was summed up in the phrase that (apart from Caesar) 'there [was] another king' (Acts 17:7) but they did not stop at proclamation. They went on to demonstrate some of the practical areas over which this King ruled—sickness, demons and even death. This mandate, to proclaim *and* demonstrate, has never been revoked nor changed, and the end of Mark's Gospel explains that the disciples proclaimed the good news and experienced God confirming their words through supernatural signs (Mark 16:20).

The church—past

The book of Acts gives us a vivid picture of a supernatural church which was committed to mission. Luke sets the scene with Jesus instructing the disciples to wait in Jerusalem until they had received power, so that they might fulfil their commission. He described this commission in terms of the ever-widening sphere of the church's mission—firstly to their home base (Jerusalem) and finally 'to the ends of the earth' (Acts 1:8). Luke then picks up the story of the church's mission. Jerusalem is impacted with the gospel and miraculous signs— 'Everyone was filled with awe, and many wonders and miraculous signs were done by the apostles' (Acts 2:43). Judea is touched also by the power of God as the reputation of this church spreads. It is genuinely hard to imagine the scene which Luke describes in chapter 5, verses 12 to 16, but when the sick were being healed by Peter's shadow it is not surprising that many sick and demonised people were brought to Jerusalem from the Judean villages for healing.

From this base the church spread (with the help of some persecution—Acts 8:2) throughout Judea and Samaria. In Samaria the evangelist Philip saw a great move of the Spirit of God which was accompanied by remarkable signs and wonders (Acts 8:4–8). Luke marks the end of a phase with his words in Acts

9:31: 'Then the church throughout Judea, Galilee and Samaria enjoyed a time of peace . . . it grew in numbers, living in the fear of the Lord.'

This summary marks the end of a very successful stage of outreach, yet the Gentiles and the wider Roman world had not really been impacted. Luke begins to set the scene for the next major phase of outreach with his record of Saul of Tarsus' conversion, Peter's contact with the Gentile world and then the exciting account of the birth of the church at Antioch (Acts 11:19–26). It was at Antioch that the believers were first called Christians, because their only distinction was that they were followers of Christ. They were now no longer a Jewish sect who believed that Messiah had come, but converts without any Jewish background.[1] In one sense they were the first-fruits of the great harvest of people from every language group which one day will stand before God's throne (Rev. 7:9).

Throughout the mission of the church signs and wonders were present. We have already noted that they were a central feature of the impact the church made on Jerusalem, Judea and Samaria and it should be no surprise to us that they continue to hallmark the mission to the Gentiles. Paul and Barnabas were able to recount the miraculous signs that God had done among the Gentiles (Acts 15:12), and even when Paul was shipwrecked on Malta he was able to hold an impromptu time of supernatural ministry (Acts 28:8–9). The miraculous was a clear dimension of the ministry of the early church—perhaps because they were so committed

---

1. The church at Antioch was not connected to a synagogue and the believers appeared not to observe the various food-laws which would have made fellowship between Jew and Gentile impossible. The Christians at Jerusalem who were Jews by background normally continued to observe the law, and so Christians were often seen as simply another Jewish sect (Acts 21:21–25), but at Antioch the *only* distinction was that they followed the Christ—hence the name Christian was given to them first at Antioch.

to the mission of reaching the world for Jesus (Rom. 15:18–19).

The church—future

Too many people talk about the good old days and as Christians we sometimes fall into the same trap. However, I believe God is committed to helping us find genuine faith and hope for the future. Scripture gives us considerable scope for optimism regarding the future and a supernatural church. Jesus indicated that we can expect a supernatural gospel to touch all the people groups of our world, for in reply to a question regarding the end of the age Jesus said: 'This gospel of the kingdom will be preached in the whole world as a testimony to all nations, and then the end will come' (Matt. 24:14).

Although this verse is subject to different interpretations, we need to ask what the original disciples would have understood by Jesus' words. Surely they would have thought in terms of the gospel of proclamation and demonstration which Jesus had inaugurated (indicated by Jesus' use of the words '*this* gospel'). For them this meant that the gospel would be proclaimed with accompanying signs, and for us it can bear no other meaning. God is still committed to sending His church across the world with a gospel of power. Jesus has not changed—He desires to continue His mission of doing and teaching in every generation.

Psalm 2 is a prophetic psalm which ultimately finds its fulfilment in the person of Jesus. As Jesus ascends the throne of heaven God speaks and promises Him the nations for His inheritance (Ps. 2:8). Jesus is to receive an inheritance which will be in proportion to the horrific sufferings which He has endured. The nations and kingdoms of this world which were claimed by Satan (Luke 4:6) are going to be given to Jesus. A final cry will go up, 'The kingdom of this world has become the kingdom of our Lord and of his Christ' (Rev. 11:15). This does not mean that the entire world will become Christian, for Scripture would seem to indicate that the light will become lighter while the darkness becomes even darker. It does, however, give us considerable genuine hope for the future. When God finally winds up this age we will be part of a great company of people who will have been redeemed from all national and language backgrounds. The church must march onwards with a supernatural gospel of power.

If the church is to fulfil its task and commission without compromise, it should not surprise us to discover that it is not the church in its *current* state which will do this. God has a plan to bring His church to maturity so that it will be comparable even to Christ Himself (Eph. 4:11–13). This, fundamentally, is why I am optimistic concerning signs and wonders and the future. We can look back and see the dimension of power displayed through the disciples and the early church; but we can also look forward and, with eyes of enlightened faith, see a similar dimension of power released in order to complete the task which the first church began with such commitment and enthusiasm.

Paul fully proclaimed the gospel from Jerusalem to Albania (Illyricum) in twelve short years (Rom. 15:19) with the aid of signs and wonders.[2] As the church regains commitment, God will bring maturity and will release the supernatural, enabling it to fulfil its mission.

---

2. Paul's first missionary journey, which begins in Acts 13, commenced around AD 46 and his letter to the Romans was written around AD 58.

If this is the future scenario then how should we respond? Should we simply sit back passively and wait for the heavens to open? A passive response will not suffice, for it is always those with genuine spiritual aggression who gain hold of the issues of the kingdom of God (Matt. 11:12). We need to be faithful with the little, while following hard after God for more. If we are to see the fulfilment of the will of God regarding the supernatural, it might be helpful to consider some of the steps that we can take in preparation.

Ground to gain

For around 1600 years the church has compromised on the supernatural and, as a result, we have ground to gain in this respect. This is further compounded by Western culture which has traditionally been scientific and rational. 'I'll believe it if I see it' might be Western and logical, but it is not a biblical confession of faith. We all want reality, and faith is certainly not claiming things took place which did not in fact happen, but a propensity to unbelief is something which we will need to deal with. Cynicism is no better than credulity.

Perhaps, though, the real battle is not against the powers 'out there', but against the personal difficulties we face. Passivity claims the lives of so many Christians, rendering them useless for God's purposes. Alongside this is the desire we all have for success. If God were to promise us nothing but success, I am sure we would then be very keen to get on and pray for sick people. However, there is no such guarantee—in fact quite the reverse. A certain amount of failure is often part of the price of pioneering in any area for the Lord.

Nothing comes automatically, and I am often

reminded of those who pioneered for a new church culture in the early 1970s. They pioneered for a church where gossip did not take place and committed relationships were the order of the day. I am the beneficiary of that today—but someone paid a price for it: they experienced failure as well as success along the way. Through the price they paid a new church culture began to grow, and many features of normal church experience today were unknown twenty or thirty years ago.

The supernatural is exactly the same—it will not come automatically. A new church culture needs to be formed where supernatural events will take place easily: a church culture where the supernatural will be accepted as normal. Like the pioneers of the last generation we need to be asking whether the attitude of our church to the supernatural matches up to Scripture or not. If not, we will need to be radical and pursue God in spite of failure.

Most of us like to live lives which are free of disappointment. Yet I have discovered that this is incompatible with seeking to please God. There *are* disappointments when we try to do the will of God and fail. I can remember praying for a person with epilepsy many years ago. It was the first person with that disease I had ever prayed for. A number of months later I heard that he had subsequently died in an epileptic fit. That was very hard for me to take. Around a year after hearing this news I was in a church in South London and the Spirit of God was moving with power. A lady came forward and asked for prayer for diabetes and epilepsy. After the meeting I was unable to find her to counsel her to continue taking the medicine—in fact I assumed that she would continue to do this and therefore didn't really think any more about that aspect of the meeting. Two weeks later I found out that she had flushed away all the medicine that same night. Obviously she was healed, and looking back now I see that God overruled, so that I would discover that He does heal epilepsy and that He could heal even through my prayers.

Through this and many other situations I have come to realise that God wants us to lay our lives down, living with our disappointments but continuing to push forward. I have discovered such joy in doing the will of God, but also a measure of disappointment, pain and frustration. If we want to live a disappointment-free life, then the supernatural will not take place for us. This, again, is an area in our church culture which must change.

God is looking for a passionate people who will be radical enough to say at every turn that church life has to adjust in order to fit in with God and His word. Nothing comes automatically, but God is longing to send His Holy Spirit with power to all who will seek to create the culture in their own lives and in their churches to receive the supernatural. I believe that, as the years unfold, healing will become much more widespread: but I am also aware that we need to prepare now for God's tomorrow.

A supernatural church

If we believe that God wants a supernatural church, we need to define what we mean by that. If our expectations are not clear, then we will be unsure as to what we are aiming at. As I read the Bible there seem to me to be two distinct strands which run through it. The first is that the supernatural is open to all. If we use Mark 16:18 as our basis for healing, then anyone with hands who is a believer qualifies for a healing ministry. A supernatural church must have this dimension of the body functioning and releasing the supernatural power of God.

There is, however, a second strand running through Scripture which is evident in the book of Acts, where the major signs and wonders were done through the hands of the apostles or other mature ministries (eg Acts 2:43; 5:12; 14:3; 15:12; 19:11). These two strands are not in opposition to each other, but need to be held in tension. If we deny people the opportunity of moving in the supernatural, then we will be making it elitist and exclusive: it will remain as a mystery to most Christians. But if we fail to recognise those whom God has anointed we will be denying God's method of maturing the body through the ministry gifts (Eph. 4:11–16).

So the supernatural is open to all believers, but we will expect to see some individuals whom God anoints in a special way for the ministry. A supernatural church will contain both elements, and will be active in creating a faith environment where Jesus can perform the miracles that He wants to.

This faith environment is at the heart of a supernatural church, because we know that it was such a key factor for Jesus and His ministry. When Jesus came to His home town, He could not do any miracles there because of the lack of faith within that community (Mark 6:5–6). Jesus required a community of faith in order to see miracles occur, and there is no reason to assume it is any different today. One of the major tasks we face in this nation is to produce church communities of faith, where Jesus can perform His miracles.

So, at the heart of a supernatural church is a community of faith. However, it is not enough for us to sit around and complain that we do not have such communities, for in that same Scripture is a resounding challenge to us all. Although Jesus could not do any miracles we also read that in spite of the unbelief, He could 'lay his hands on a few sick people and heal them' (Mark 6:5). The challenge remains for us to begin to lay our hands on a few sick people and see them recover. As we see a few small healing miracles take place, it will help to move the church forward to a stronger place of faith for greater miracles.

We don't know what miracles Jesus was able to perform and which ones He was not on that occasion, but I have noticed that certain miracles are often listed together: the blind receiving their sight; the lame walking; the deaf receiving their hearing back; the dumb being healed; and the dead being raised. I suspect that it was these miracles which Jesus was unable to perform on that day. Even if we find that miracles in that category are beyond our experience, it still leaves us sufficient scope to get on with!

In my own experience, I have noticed, during the years that I have been praying for those who are sick, a steady increase in 'results'. I am sure this is due in part to my own faith growing, but also to the faith-for-miracles in the church community increasing. It is building this faith culture which is so important if we are to see Jesus perform the miracles that He loves to do.

I hope that by now we are beginning to see that the supernatural will not occur automatically, but that we need to work with the Holy Spirit so that a suitable environment for God to move in is created. Thank God, though, it is not simply down to us—He is working with us, and is committed to releasing a supernatural gospel through a supernatural church to the nations of this world.

A faith culture

If the supernatural will not occur automatically we will need to begin to take steps within our churches to facilitate it. It will need to come onto the agenda in a new way for many churches. I am sure that in many churches and leaders' meetings there has never been any discussion, and probably very little prayer, surrounding the area of the supernatural.

Teaching plays a very important role in changing a church culture, and over the past few years the church of which I am a part has held various seminars and workshops on such subjects as prophecy, healing and the supernatural, to begin to educate people and raise the level of faith and expectancy. If we are inexperienced then I would recommend that we seek to learn from those who are seeing some success in this sphere. I have read very widely on the subject and have sat in meetings where people have been moving in the supernatural power of God. I cannot say I have been able to agree with everything I have read, and I have certainly not liked everything I have seen, but it has helped to stretch me and take me on a step or two. We must never be afraid of learning from others—even from those who have a different persuasion from ourselves.

Finally, in creating a faith culture we will need to commit ourselves to getting involved in praying for others. This is vital. I know of one pastor who was asked how he had received his ministry for healing, and his reply was that he had committed himself to pray for the first 200 sick people that God brought across his path. There comes a point where we need to step out. It might be that we will need someone to help us get started, but at some stage we will have to take it up for ourselves.

I first began praying for those who were sick in 1984. I started by asking God to bring across my path one sick person per week for me to pray with. I wanted to learn from my failures as well as my successes. Later I asked God for three people a week, and God was faithful to me. I have discovered He is faithful to teach and train us even if there appear to be so few opportunities.

CHAPTER 2

A BIBLICAL FRAMEWORK

At the last count I had around forty books on my shelves which cover the Bible's teaching on healing, and I am very aware that many of those authors express different viewpoints on the subject. Quite a number of them have excellent healing ministries, and therefore it is with some caution that I am approaching this chapter. For these reasons I am simply calling this chapter 'a', not 'the', biblical framework, because I wish to acknowledge that there are other legitimate ways in which to approach Scripture.

If we are to be involved in healing it is important that we have a rationale for our beliefs and convictions. As in every other area of the Christian life we are not to form our theology from our experience, or even from our own wistful desires. Our theology must be based firmly on Scripture. Healing can be a very emotive subject, particularly when the issue of those who have not been healed is raised. These questions are not simply restricted to our own experience, but also apply to some of the situations which appear in the Bible—for example, what do we make of Paul and his 'thorn in the flesh'?[1] Whenever healing is discussed both theological and pastoral questions are raised, but it is important that we devote ourselves firstly to the theological issues.

1. Paul's thorn in the flesh is discussed in Appendix 1 at the close of this book.

Theologically there are those who, to one degree or another, use a dispensational-type argument to explain why we should not expect to see healing in great abundance, or even at all, in church life today.[2] They may do this in an extreme fashion where they claim that healing was for the apostolic era and that it died out with those first-generation apostles. Thankfully there are no serious scholars (certainly in this country) who now take this approach, but there remains a more subtle form of this theology, with those who claim that Scripture shows that miracles are clumped together around certain individuals and in certain eras of history. This, they claim, is as a result of the sovereignty of God and so the miraculous might still be our experience on rare occasions, but we should not expect to see miracles in great abundance. They will continue to be the exception rather than the rule.

Alongside this is the rather depressing and faith-killing attitude that there is really very little we can do to promote or release healing. To pray 'the prayer of faith' is to pray with full assurance that whatever takes place will be the best in this situation. Such prayers do not need a lot of faith, and I am glad that James illustrates the prayer of faith with the life of Elijah, who refused to accept the status quo but prayed earnestly that it would not rain on the basis of his words (James 5:17, 18; 1 Kings 17:1). Elijah had no passive faith in God—he was active and really believed his prayers made a difference.

At the other extreme are those who teach in as many words that we should 'name it and claim it'. They teach

---

2. Dispensationalism is the term which is commonly applied to the system of biblical interpretation which was popularised by the *Scofield Study Bible*. Under this method of interpretation, the history of the world was divided into different dispensations and it was commonly taught that God dealt with His people differently in each dispensation. When this was applied to healing, this extreme form of interpretation believed that healing died out with the apostolic era.

that healing comes to all who have faith, and so if a person is not healed it is simply due to their lack of faith. Once a person believes for healing only the symptoms can persist, not the actual sickness itself. I often comment that it is a shame that the symptoms cause as many problems as the original sickness!

It needs to be said that from the latter school have come some tremendous stories of dynamic miracles, and I have often been very impressed by their aggressive faith. I would rather opt for their positive approach than the former position of a passive faith in the sovereignty of God. I *do* believe in the sovereignty of God but not as outlined in that view. Prayer *does* make a difference—we can change the way things are. However, having expressed my appreciation for the faith school I also need to point out that this simple faith approach does not take into consideration all the biblical data, and is too neat a package when we approach the subject of healing.

There are certain premises which should be established from the outset. It is almost certain that there was no sickness present in mankind prior to the Fall. We know that the entrance of sin had cosmic repercussions, and one result is the presence of sickness in human experience. So in a very real sense we can say that sickness is 'from the devil', but we must not then make the mistake of assuming that every sickness is therefore the result of personal sin. Jesus made this clear when the disciples asked Him about the man who was born blind. They assumed that personal sin had to be involved in this situation, but Jesus was emphatic that personal sin was *not* involved.[3] There is a narrow line along which we

---

3. John 9:3 can sound very harsh in many of our translations, (e.g. NIV) as if God had inflicted this man with blindness *in order to* reveal His power, but this is not the only possible translation. It could be the 'imperatival hina' and better translated as a positive statement from Jesus, 'but let the work of God be manifested'. This would then be in keeping with Jesus' response to sickness.

There are times when personal sin can cause sickness, whether as a result of cause and effect or punishment from God, but great care needs to be taken when making such statements.

must walk, for Jesus also clearly saw sickness as an enemy which needed to be rebuked.[4] So sickness is not the sign of the presence of personal sin, but it is a demonstration of the presence of the kingdom of darkness in human affairs. It is a sign that the will of God is not yet here in its fullness.

God is King

There is a theme running throughout Scripture which is probably the best framework to adopt when considering the area of healing. It is the framework of God and His kingship. God is proclaimed as King in the Old Testament and yet there was also a sense in which He was still to become king.[5] This theme of God's kingship or rule is continued in the New Testament, and given even greater definition and centrality, for it is in the New Testament that we come across the phrase 'the kingdom of God'.[6]

Although there are different interpretations of this phrase, Jesus clearly taught that the kingdom of God was already here, and yet it was still to come.[7] For Jesus,

4. When Jesus came to pray with Peter's mother-in-law He rebuked the fever (Luke 4:39). This may have been because He detected the presence of a spirit behind this disease. There are several occasions recorded in the Gospels where Jesus attributed illness directly to the work of a demon and therefore rebuked the demon. Whatever the reason was in this particular situation, it certainly highlights the fact that He attacked illness and expressed anger when confronted by it.

5. So, for example, Psalm 47:2 states that God is 'the great King over all the earth'; and Psalm 2:4 describes God as 'the One enthroned in heaven'. These Scriptures describe God as King.
    Other Old Testament Scriptures describe God as yet to become king, so for example Zechariah 14:9: 'The Lord will be king over all the earth. On that day there will be one Lord . . .'

6. Both the Hebrew and Greek words behind this phrase (*malekuth* and *basileia* respectively) convey the sense of 'reign' or 'rule' rather than the more static term of 'realm'. Matthew tends to use the term 'kingdom of heaven' simply because he was writing for Jews, who avoided using the term 'God' or 'Yahweh' for fear of blaspheming and therefore often replaced those names with such terms as 'heaven'.

7. There are many excellent books about the kingdom of God. Perhaps the person who has contributed most to an evangelical understanding of the kingdom in recent decades is George Ladd, and I recommend his works for those who wish to pursue this vital study, especially *A Theology of the New Testament* (Lutterworth Press, 1975) and *The Gospel of the Kingdom* (Eerdmans, 1959) which cover the subject in more detail than we can here. *Power Evangelism* by John Wimber and Kevin Springer (Hodder & Stoughton, 1985) also covers the theme; and there is an excellent treatise by the South African charismatic Derek Morphew, *Breakthrough* (Struick Books, 1991).

God's kingdom was already here in measure but would only come in fullness at the close of this age. That kingdom will be fully expressed when Jesus returns and 'the kingdom of the world has become the kingdom of our Lord and of his Christ' (Rev. 11:15).

This theme of the kingdom of God being already here but not yet in its fullness is merely the outworking of the Old Testament concept of God as King. God's rule is already here, and we have already tasted of the powers of the coming age (Heb. 6:5); yet His rule is still to be fully established and expressed on earth in the future. When the end comes there will be no more sickness nor sadness, for sin and all its effects will finally have been dealt with. However, the gospel message (or Good News) is that we do not have to wait until then to taste some of the benefits of the redemption that one day will be ours in fullness. When Jesus comes again our bodies will receive such an almighty touch from heaven that they will be totally transformed (1 Cor. 15:52): healing is simply a foretaste now of that resurrection power.

Signposts pointing in two directions

Jesus saw the supernatural as a sign of the presence of His kingdom (Matt. 12:28). When asked about His Messianic credentials, He told John's disciples to report the miracles they had seen Him perform because the miracles were signs that His kingdom was present (Matt. 11:5–6). They indicated that the 'year of the Lord's favour' was already here (Luke 4:17–21). This then seems the best way to understand healing in the church today. Miracles still demonstrate the presence of His kingdom. They are signs which point in two directions. They point backwards to the decisive blow which Jesus delivered to the devil when He died and rose again. From that point our future was certain—God's kingdom will one day rule over all. From that time on, Jesus had all authority in heaven and in earth.[8] Miracles also point forward to the day when there will be no more need for healing because sickness (and death) will finally have been abolished. They point forward to the day when our bodies will be finally and completely transformed. Miracles are then a sign of the presence of Jesus' rule and reign, and the more that Jesus is allowed to rule and reign the more we can expect to see the miraculous in evidence. Miracles are not the only sign of the presence of His kingdom, but they are a major one.

This rule must touch every area of our life—our morality, relationships, priorities, mind-sets and unbelief. Healing will not be automatic in every case, but our experience of success will be greatly increased the more Jesus is allowed to rule without any parameters.

The Bible presents us with a battle theology. It is a book about war between Satan and mankind from beginning to end. The issue of who will rule is a key one which we will need to understand if we are to grapple with some of the real issues we have to face in our world today. Healing will not be automatic because it is one of the arenas where many battles are fought. These battles are sometimes won and sometimes lost. However, for the Christian, there can be no ultimate defeat, for our destiny is secure: death is on the one hand the final enemy, but it is also the only barrier between us and a life of fulfilment which is waiting for us on the other side of the grave. Sometimes Christians do die prematurely through sickness, but even then there is no ultimate defeat

8. Jesus' words in Matt. 28:18 are dynamite. Ever since creation the issue has been 'Who will rule in the earth?' Mankind was given authority to rule on God's behalf, but foolishly gave that authority to Satan who has abused his authority ever since. Jesus rose from the dead, making it clear that His authority included the territory originally given to mankind.

because Jesus has defeated death itself.[9]

Healing: frequent or occasional?

If healings and miracles are a sign of the presence of God's rule, should we expect them to be occasional signs or a very normal part of our experience? The simplest way to answer this is to ask the question this way round: if Jesus were here today in physical form what would He be involved in? I am sure we will all agree that a major part of His activity would involve the supernatural, and we know from reading the Gospel records that He never refused to heal anyone. In fact some astounding statements are made including the following: He healed all who came to Him; He healed all who touched Him; all who touched the hem of His garment were healed.[10] His response to sickness was always the same—He healed sick people wherever He went.

He also commissioned the disciples, expecting them to carry out the same work. In a nutshell, they were to proclaim the presence of the kingdom of God and then to demonstrate it in a very practical way, through healing the sick, casting out demons and raising the dead. These supernatural acts were signs for Jesus that the kingdom of God was at hand, and they were also signs for the early church of the presence of the kingdom of God. As we saw in the last chapter, nothing has changed—Jesus still wants to act and teach in the same way as always.

---

9. In 1 Corinthians 11:30 Paul says that some of the believers there had died before their time because they had not 'recognised the body of the Lord'. This might have a dual application to the Lord's physical body and to the church as the body of Christ, although it is an unusual way for Paul to describe the church—he normally uses the term the 'body of Christ' when referring to the church.

   We also have a record of a number of people in the New Testament who died and were raised from the dead, which surely indicates that they had died prematurely.

10. There are some remarkable statements about the healings of Jesus and the large numbers that He healed. Look up some of the following references—Matt. 4:23–25; 8:16; 9:35–38; 12:15; 14:14; 15:29–31; 19:2; 21:14; Mark 6:54–56.

I would like to suggest that this framework of the kingdom of God is the best one with which to look at the subject of healing in the Bible. Jesus is King, and his kingdom is present for all to respond to: the evidence of His kingship is through healing and deliverance.

This means that the greater the manifestation of His kingdom, the more we can expect to see the supernatural, and in a very real sense we can confidently state that it is the will of God to heal. This statement is not to be taken to mean that all we pray for will be healed, but it is meant to state boldly that if Jesus were present physically, and He laid hands on them, they would be healed. This then must be both our starting point for our understanding of healing and also the goal at which we are aiming. We cannot rest satisfied until we see God's kingdom come in all its fullness. We will continue to strain after a greater manifestation of His kingdom's rule and, although we know that we also need to wait until He comes again before that rule is totally expressed, we can look at the early church and be inspired to reach out after more in the here and now.[11]

It is actually true that healings are clumped around certain figures and eras in history. This is because wherever God is allowed to reign, His power can be released. This should challenge us to see miracles clumped around our churches and in our generation.

Corporate faith

The challenge before us is to demonstrate the presence of the kingdom of God in the same way that Jesus and the

---

11. As in the Gospels and their references to the ministry of Jesus, there are also similar references to the miracles that were present in the early church. Acts 5:12–16; 9:11; 28:8–9 all describe the extent of the miraculous. It seems that they proclaimed the message, believed God and He confirmed their message (Mark 16:20; Acts 14:3).

early church did. However, even Jesus was limited by unbelief. When He came to His home town He was unable to perform certain miracles there because of their unbelief (Mark 6:1–6; Matt. 13:53–58). Jesus needed a community of faith in order to release some key miracles, and we will soon find that if He needed such a community, then we will too, even more so. The church is to be that community of faith where Jesus can come and perform the miracles which He still loves to do.

The Bible is not explicit about the exact nature of what occurred on that day but we do read that Jesus was unable to 'do any miracles there, except lay his hands on a few sick people and heal them' (Mark 6:5). He was able to heal a few sick people, but unable to move beyond this. From the context it seems that there was a category of more spectacular miracles that He was unable to perform on that day. It was not that His will had changed—Scripture makes it quite clear that He was disappointed and unable to do any more because of the lack of faith He discovered at that time.

The challenge which we face is to begin to lay our hands on a few sick people and see them recover, while continuing to work with the church communities of which we are a part until they become communities of faith which allow Jesus to do whatever He chooses. So we must be very careful about making the assumption that it is not the will of God to heal someone if we experience that they have not been healed in response to prayer.

The power of the Spirit

The Holy Spirit is vital if we are to see people healed. Jesus told His disciples to wait in Jerusalem until they had received power, and He Himself did not perform any miracles until He was anointed by the power of the Spirit, because He was dependent upon that anointing to heal.[12] God loves to heal, but we too have a part to play in that healing work. We will need to be endued with God's power, and our churches need to become places where genuine faith is high. Then I believe we will begin to see some 'extraordinary miracles' take place (Acts 19:11).

There is much debate over the will of God and healing, but I think there is a point on which all honest readers of the New Testament can agree. In the light of Scripture I think it is easy to acknowledge that if the will of God was being fulfilled in every situation, then many more would be healed than are currently healed. So if that is the case we can and should be praying that the kingdom of God will come with power, and we do not need to live with the conclusion that our current experience is therefore the expression of the will of God. We should readily acknowledge that we do not understand all aspects of healing and that God is working on a far bigger canvas than we ever do, but this does not in any way contradict our understanding of the heart and will of God to heal.

Jesus' promise to His disciples was that they would do the same works that He had been doing and even greater works (John 14:12). We cannot afford to hide behind a comfortable theology of the sovereignty of God and the mystery of His will if we are going to take the Great Commission seriously. There are theological issues which need to be understood: God does sometimes hold back on giving something good because He knows more than we do; we do live with the tension of waiting until Jesus comes, before all His enemies will be made His

---

12. Luke records that the 'power of the Lord was present for him to heal the sick' (Luke 5:17), indicating that Jesus was dependent upon that anointing.

footstool—but we also have confidence that the kingdom of God has come near and we have been commissioned to demonstrate its presence and reality.

Abraham and his choice

There are many other Scriptures that we could look at, and I suggest that anyone who has a desire to move in healing familiarise themselves with the passages of Scripture which speak of healing. We do not have space to analyse them all here, but there is one Old Testament story of healing which has stood out for me in recent years. It is the story of Abraham, Sarah and Abimelech (Gen. 20). Abraham eventually has to pray for all the women who are associated with Abimelech's household, for they had all become infertile. As a result of Abraham's prayers they are healed. The significance of the story lies in the fact that it is Abraham who has to pray. Abraham has a promise from God which has not been fulfilled (that his barren wife will give birth to a son) and he faces the enormous challenge of either believing his experience or trusting God's word. This is a situation which we will find ourselves in many times over, and the choice we will need to make is exactly the same as the choice which Abraham faced—do we believe God's word or live by our experience?

Our theology must be based on God's word and not on our experience. There are pastoral issues to be faced but only after we lay this firm foundation of theology, otherwise we will continually bring everything down to our own experience. Genesis 21:1 begins with a very significant three-letter word: 'now'. Only after Abraham's step of obedience, in spite of his past experience, did God give to Sarah the fulfilment of the promise.

Is healing in the atonement?

This is a common question which can be misleading and unfortunate. If by this we mean that Jesus died on the cross to break the power of the enemy over human affairs then the answer must be in the affirmative. Surely all God's blessings come to us through the sufferings of Jesus and this must include healing.[13]

If, however, by this question we mean that healing is therefore ours to be demanded from God whenever we choose, the answer would have to be 'no'. Much of this is resolved, though, when we have a fuller understanding of the atonement. Christ died not simply to set us free from sin in this age but ultimately to reconcile all things to God. His death has a cosmic effect because it impacts everything which sin has affected. He has died, but this does not make everything automatic and immediate. At times God holds back for a purpose, but this does not mean that we are left in the dark when it comes to praying for sick people. Jesus lived, died and rose again so that we might be free from all the damage of the

---

13. There is a very strong argument to see healing as being part of the 'package' of blessing that results from the death of Jesus. Matthew quotes Isaiah 53:4 in the context of the healing ministry of Jesus (Matt. 8:16–17) and Peter likewise quotes the Isaiah passage in 1 Peter 2:24. There he uses the word *iaomai* (healed) which is always used of physical healing elsewhere in the New Testament. I am more comfortable with the understanding that healing comes to us because Jesus died and therefore *through* the atonement, rather than describing healing as being *in* the atonement. Part of the problem arises through seeing the atonement as some sort of exact legal payment which then purchases healing or forgiveness for us, rather than as a substituted death to redeem everything which sin has affected.

Sin and sickness belong to two different categories. Sickness is not sin but is a consequence of sin: it carries no penalty therefore cannot be atoned for in the same way as sin. This is why it is better to state that healing can come to us through the atonement but is not present in the atoning work of Christ directly.

Some have used 1 Peter 2:24 to suggest that Jesus bore our sicknesses when He was scourged ('by his wounds you have been healed') and that He bore our sins when He died on the cross. However, the word translated as 'wounds' (*molops*) in 1 Peter 2:24 is in the singular and is not the normal word for the marks of a whip. It is interesting to note that healing was offered by the early church on the basis of the power and authority of Jesus and there is no mention of them offering healing on the basis of Christ's death, whereas they clearly offered forgiveness on that basis. For these reasons I am far more comfortable in holding to the view that the blessings of God come through the sufferings of Christ, but that it is misleading to state that healing is in the atonement.

enemy. We continue to pray positively towards that end, accepting that we live in the tension that the kingdom is already here in part, but will one day come in full power.

One day there will be no more sickness and only health; today we pray for healing. One day there will be no more decay as our bodies will be redeemed and regenerated; today we look for His quickening power to bring life to our mortality. There is an ageing process, but this does not invalidate belief in healing, any more than belief in healing is a denial of the death process which is taking place in us.

Holding together these tensions is vital if we are to help people through the pastoral situations which we all have to face when people are not healed. We can, however, approach it positively and use such situations to help produce maturity in our corporate relationship with the Lord.

Conclusive proof?

The supernatural is not something which gives conclusive proof that God is alive. Many saw the supernatural power at work through Jesus, yet did not accept Him. God is not interested in proving that He exists to those who are not open to Him, but He wants us to be involved in the work of the kingdom, so that many who are open-hearted can find God to be alive and interested in them. Matthew records Jesus making a very strong statement regarding Sodom when He claimed that repentance would have come to that city if it could have seen the miracles that Capernaum had seen (Matt. 11:20–24). This should challenge us all to seek God for miracles that will bring whole cities and communities to repentance.

It is interesting to note that although Capernaum did

see the miracles, it still did not repent. This highlights the fact that when people have closed their minds (often through religion), nothing will actually convince them of the power of God. But for honest 'unbelievers' Jesus said that miracles are a real key in seeing them won to God.

The challenges before us are enormous. It is not simply the challenge of producing good theology, but the far greater one of demonstrating the presence of God's kingdom. The choice is ours regardless of our theology—will we bring Scripture into line with our experience or will we, by God's grace, continue to try to bring our experience into line with Scripture?

CHAPTER 3

PASTORAL PERSPECTIVES

Healing can cause a number of pastoral difficulties and there are some common objections which are raised whenever healing is discussed. I want to look at some of them in this chapter, to give us a good foundation before we discuss some of the practical areas involved in praying with people in the next chapter.

Sickness and suffering

The Christian faith never shrinks back from the real issues which we face in life. Suffering is part of the fallen world in which we live, and indeed Christians are told to expect to suffer in this world. No one who reads the Bible with an open mind can escape from that fact. With this as a backdrop, there are those who argue that sickness is part of the suffering process and, as with all suffering, God has a purpose which is normally to perfect us through producing Godly character in us.

There is no question that many Godly people who have been very ill have discovered God in new ways through their illness. God uses every opportunity to teach and equip us but the main question we must ask is—does the Bible teach that we are sanctified through sickness? Perhaps the most surprising fact is that although the

Bible does talk about suffering, it never once includes sickness under the category of suffering.[1] The New Testament teaches us to endure suffering but to pray that God will heal us when we are sick (James 5:13–16).

Instinctively we know that sickness is not part of the will of God for humanity, because we all applaud the medical world when they work hard to alleviate sickness. In fact if we are sick we will often go to the doctor in order to find healing. If God was seeking to sanctify us through this particular sickness we would find ourselves in the embarrassing position of working against the purposes of God!

I am not seeking to argue that God will not use sickness, nor that we can understand every mystery. I am simply asking that we make sure we base our theology and understanding firmly on the revelation of God as we find it in the Bible.

Not everyone is healed

The above statement is as obviously true today as it was in biblical times, but we must be careful not to base our theology on our experience. It might also be possible to observe that not everyone receives salvation, or that not all the famines in the world are relieved, but we would be foolish then to insist, on the basis of our observations, that the will of God is to leave some people unsaved and allow the millions who starve simply to die.

---

1. Ken Blue picks up on this point in his book *The Authority to Heal* (Monarch, 1989), particularly in pages 25–28. He points out that the Greek word *pascho* (to suffer) and its derivatives occur 65 times and that the Greek word-group *thlipsis* (affliction) occurs 55 times. Of the 120 references not one of them refers to physical sickness. It seems that the vocabulary attached to suffering is limited in the New Testament to external pressure or persecution and is applied to the work of people, demons or even the judgement of God, but never to illness.

I often find that people are reticent to ask for prayer for healing because of the questions of self-worth that might be raised if they are not healed. If doctors do not produce a cure, then we are all aware that they are finite and do not have all the answers. In such a case we do not take it personally. God, however, has all power and if He does not heal us it can raise the question in our mind that perhaps He does not want to heal us, because there is something wrong with us, and so He has chosen to reject or ignore us.

We need to have realistic expectations when we approach the subject of healing. The Bible talks about healing and not regeneration for us in this present age. There is a death process already taking place in our bodies and I will therefore be physically unable to do at the age of seventy-five what I could do at the age of fifteen. However, this does not mean that I should expect to grow old and become totally immobile. God wants me to fulfil the purposes He has for me on this earth, and I can expect to find the necessary physical refreshment from Him to fulfil this.

It is easy to talk about healing and the need to base our theology on Scripture, but we must never forget that healing has to do with people. It is this pastoral aspect which needs to be present as we deal with those who are sick, otherwise we might damage many people in the name of good theology.

Pastoral issues

Those who pray have a responsibility to help those sick who are looking to God for healing to work through any areas of disappointment and guilt. We must take the pressure off people so that they do not feel they are on trial and end up either guilty or disappointed if they are not healed. We need an understanding of theology, of how God operates, but also we need an understanding of people. I am constantly amazed and challenged by the way Jesus approached those who were sick. He found out exactly where they were and met them at *their* point of need.

We need to be honest when we come to pray for people and let them see us and our vulnerability, so that they realise that all the responsibility does not lie with them. Let's be honest—the major difference between the New Testament and today is with those who pray and not with those who are being prayed with. Sick people have not changed but those who pray have!

We will also need to exercise wisdom about the people we pray with and how we pray with them. One of the worst scenarios I have discovered is at the end of a meeting when some poor person has been dragged up for me to pray with. Their friend is highly enthusiastic and 'in faith', but the actual person is wishing the ground would open up. In those situations it is very difficult to pray for healing so I would rather reassure the person that Jesus accepts them and then pray for the blessing of God on them. We must treat people as individuals and not be on a mission to prove our theology right. We will not be judged, on the final day, on the basis of our theology, but on the basis of how we responded to Christ and to humanity.

Death is a taboo subject in the twentieth-century Western world, yet it is the most certain fact of life! We should not be involved in praying for the sick simply to stop them from dying, but rather we need to be able to handle the tension of believing God for healing and also the very real fact of death. Death is not a tragedy for the Christian, and we need to develop a positive theology of death and dying as well as healing and health.

There are pastoral issues which we will need to deal with, but rather than accepting them as reasons why we should avoid teaching on healing, we can find that healing becomes the very catalyst by which they can be positively addressed.

Healing and faith

There is one other area which we would do well to look at briefly and that is the connection between healing and faith. Without doubt there is a connection between the two, but I do not see it as a law which states that if I put enough of the right currency of faith in the machine I will then receive healing. We do not deal with a machine but with a Person, and faith is a description of our relationship with God, not the commodity which we use to get our will in any situation.

In the Bible Jesus healed people with different levels of faith, and so it is hard to draw up a formula which is exact in every case. However we do know that faith pleases God and that He responds to faith, so we should not assume that healing is totally independent of it. Whilst considering faith it will be good to make some brief observations about the connection between hope and faith.

In Hebrews 11:1 we read that 'faith is being sure of what we hope for'. If we are not hoping for something we will have nowhere to place our faith. Many times, faith begins simply as a sense of hope. With regard to healing it would mean that we are hoping that God will heal us, but we are not sure that He will. That is a good starting point and a very necessary one. If we continue to hope and be open to God and seek to respond to His word, we will find that often our hope changes to faith. I like to describe hope as the mould in which our faith can set. Faith is the substance but hope is the framework.

One of the best biblical illustrations is of the woman who had been haemorrhaging for twelve years and was not improving at all (Mark 5:25–34). She had begun to allow some hope to arise within her own mind and heart as she kept saying to herself (the Greek tense of the verb 'thought' in verse 28 is continuous) that if she could only touch Jesus' cloak she would be healed. I am sure she did not suddenly come to a conviction of faith in an instant, but that it began with a sense of hope. The interesting thing is that Jesus attributed this healing to the woman's faith. The mould had become filled and her faith was set.

Hope is to do with seeing the future differently; faith is knowing that God has given the answer in the present—even if the fruit of the problem still remains (Mark 11:24). Too many people try and concentrate on having enough faith (how much is enough?). Far better that we concentrate on seeing the possibilities and the answer that will take place if and when Jesus touches us. Some people give up too soon when they seek healing and cast away any sense of hope before it has changed to real faith.

There are issues to be dealt with and many of them seek to destroy any hope which we have. Often the medical opinion or our own fears speak so loudly to us that any sense of hope disappears. This is particularly true in situations where we are dealing with long-term or terminal illness. One of our tasks is to help people see that there are other possibilities through communicating acceptance and the truths of Scripture. It is in the context of acceptance and Scripture that genuine faith is developed, for it is not something which we work up but something which 'comes' as we respond to Him

(Rom. 10:17). If we get on the trip of examining how much faith we have we will soon be destroyed. It is far better to be aware of His love and acceptance, for then we will be creating an environment where faith can grow.

If we are going to pray for sick people it is important that we ourselves have a vibrant faith in the power of God, and that we continually allow God to wash our minds in the truths of Scripture. Our faith will be tested and we must know *whom* we have believed as well as *what* we have believed. Faith is important but, as has already been stated, corporate or community faith is a far bigger factor for miracles than the faith of the individual who is sick.

Bringing healing to people is a challenge to hold on to the truths of Scripture whilst seeking to treat people as individuals. We cannot reduce healing to formulas which we give to people in order that they may be healed: we must present to them a Person. There are pastoral difficulties which are thrown up when healing is taught and practised, but those questions and difficulties should simply give us an opportunity to discover the One who stands behind every healing.

Bringing healing often involves bringing people to a point where they have worked through various issues and objections. Part of the healing process is helping them to come to terms with self-acceptance, so that they are ready to receive from God. All of this needs wise handling and we need to bear in mind that God wants to bring wholeness and not simply healing. So it is important that we do not focus on healing and sickness to the exclusion of people. We will pick this up further in the next chapter as we discuss praying for those who are sick.

CHAPTER 4

PRAYING FOR PEOPLE WHO ARE SICK

It is now time to look at some of the practicalities involved in praying with people who are sick. The chapter title might be a little clumsy, but I have used it in order to emphasise that we are not simply praying for 'the sick' but for *people* who are sick. If we lose this emphasis we will be in danger of failing to express the love of Jesus for people. We might well become more concerned with our right principles than with individuals who are made in the image of God. We need to hold on to the fact that God's desire is to bring wholeness, and not simply healing, to people.

If we maintain an emphasis on praying for people, we will seek the best approach to help a person connect with God. Healing comes from God and so we can serve best by helping them to make a connection to the Living God. With this uppermost in our minds we will not simply try to foist our principles, or impose our way of doing things, onto them.

In healing there are no right formulas or right prayers, but there are certain 'parties' who all have a role to play. Firstly there is God and we need to face it—if He doesn't heal then we can't! There is really no purpose in getting uptight if God does not heal, because our annoyance will not help with the healing process! Secondly we ourselves have a part to play which, I suggest, is mainly in helping the one who is sick connect with the Lord. We are there as midwives to help with the delivery. Finally there is the person being prayed with who has a part to play as well.

As we approach this subject it is good to know that God is only too willing to make up what we lack and to cover for our many mistakes, but this should not mean that we no longer take care with our approach. Every situation is different and it is therefore important that we approach each person in need of healing with a fresh openness. I have been very impressed as I have read through the Gospels to see how many different approaches Jesus had. It appears He discovered where each person was, met them at that point and helped them to touch God for themselves.

We will soon discover how different each situation is, and in order to help people find God we will need to find out where they are and relax them. As far as possible, in a relaxed way, we need to try to create an environment of faith and expectancy. A very important element of the prayer time is for the person to receive us as someone sent from God into their situation. This is something that I would even ask someone who was not a Christian to do, for Jesus said that whoever received His disciples as those He had sent would receive Him (Matt. 10:40). If people are to receive healing from the Lord it is important that they receive us as His disciples.[1]

---

1. This was a factor which hindered Jesus when He came to His home town. They refused to receive Him as one sent from God but saw Him simply as 'the carpenter's son'. It is also a very important factor in the work of elders who come to pray in line with James 5:14–16. Elders need to know that they have been commissioned by God to look after the spiritual well-being of a church and are therefore being sent and carrying His authority. Conversely the person who has requested them to pray needs to receive them in that way as well. This is highlighted by the fact that if sin has been committed it needs to be exposed and forgiveness given. Too many times I have realised that leaders have gone wondering whether God has gifted them in healing, rather than going as delegated servants with authority. It is also sadly true that many times those who have called for them do not treat them with respect and are not prepared to submit their lives to them. This theme of sending and receiving is repeated many times in the New Testament and is a key to the release of spiritual authority.

I was invited through a mutual friend to go to the home of a young man who was very ill. He had been housebound for more than six months as he suffered from constant pain. On his better days he experienced something akin to the symptoms of extreme migraine headaches. I sat with him and his mother and explained that it was not an issue to me whether they believed in God or not, but that I did request them to accept that if there was a God then He had arranged for me to be with them on this afternoon. They agreed to that and I prayed. I opened my eyes to see both of them in tears on the settee as this God, who might or not exist, had touched them very powerfully. The next I heard of him was that he was off on a trip to the USA and his mother asked me if I would consider praying for another relative of hers. She had gained considerable ground in her position of faith, but I believe that much of it was due to the fact that they had agreed to receive me as someone sent from a God who might exist.

We are often asked to pray at inconvenient times and we need to determine if this is the right time to pray. We should pray when we are ready, not when we have been manipulated into praying—either emotionally or circumstantially. It is important that faith is present when we pray and this means that we might have to choose a time when we are ready. When Peter came to pray for Dorcas he did not focus on the problem, but spent time in the presence of God until he was ready to turn to Dorcas' body and speak to it (Acts 9:40). We are often tempted to rush in and seek to bring an answer long before we have any sense of faith for the situation at all. So we should not be embarrassed about asking to pray with the person at a later stage if we sense this is the wrong time. We might then need to spend time seeking God and preparing our own hearts in order to be ready.

Many times we will also need to determine what expectancy is present in the person who is asking for prayer. Paul saw that the man who was lame at Lystra had faith to be healed and therefore spoke a word of release to him (Acts 14:8–9). As we discover where each person is we will often need to help them through the fears and doubts which are usually present. Sometimes this process is necessary as a preliminary before we come to pray for healing.

Choosing a model for prayer

There are different ways to pray for healing. When the power of the Spirit is present we can simply give a word of command. We often read of such commands in Scripture, but we need to know that it is not the command that accomplishes the miracle—but the command that is faith-filled. When the presence of the Holy Spirit is strong the prayers can often be short, for miracles occur when the Spirit of God and the word of God come together, as is evidenced at the creation where we read that the Spirit of God hovered over the earth and then God spoke (Gen. 1:1–3).

When the Holy Spirit is not in such tangible evidence it is probably better to pray over a longer period of time and interact both with the Holy Spirit and the person. This is the 'model' which is outlined in the books on healing which John Wimber and others have written. This simply means that we spend some time initially finding out the facts. This is genuinely to establish the facts but it also prepares the person through developing trust. The next step is to invite the Holy Spirit to come and begin His work, and throughout this period we should simply pray what we hear the Holy Spirit say to us and respond to the answers the person might be giving us. Finally, after prayer, some form of post-prayer instruction often needs to be given, and perhaps even another appointment should be made for the person if there is yet more healing to be received.

In order to help remember the above steps I have labelled the process as follows: *interview* the person; *invite* the Holy Spirit to be active; *interact* both with the work of the Spirit and the person; *instruct* the person subsequent to the prayer time. Francis MacNutt and others have described this process as 'soaking prayer'.

Healing can be instantaneous (which is wonderful), or it can be a process which takes place as a result of prayer, or indeed it can be progressive where an improvement is made each time prayer is given. We cannot determine how it will take place, but we need to be ready to work with God and prepared to accept the process He is using.

As we pray it is important that people open up to the love of Jesus, and it is often good to begin by praying for the person and thanking God for them. This will begin to expose them to the love of God and, as we pray, we will often begin to pray prophetically into their situation. Through all of this we must remember our task is to help them connect with God Himself.

One of the greatest thrills for me recently was to pray for a young girl of around eleven years of age. She had suffered for around three years with a number of diseases and as a last resort the mother brought her along to my office. I spoke with the two of them for about fifteen minutes to put their minds at rest that nothing odd was going to happen. To reassure them that God still heals today I told them about other people who had been healed. I then prayed probably the simplest prayer for healing I have ever prayed. I said, 'Lord Jesus, you know

this situation. We would love you to come and heal now.'
I didn't pray any more but began talking to the girl, asking her about school and the things she liked to do with one purpose in mind. I realised that she needed to relax so that there would be an openness to God. After about ten minutes I asked her how she was doing, and she replied that she had been feeling a lot of heat go through all the joints where she had the problems. My reply was that I would not be surprised if God had healed her, but we would need to wait and see.

After she left my office, she began to swim extensively every day, as well as cycling everywhere, and the doctors (she was under a team of specialists in London) wrote across her report 'miraculous recovery'. I chose how I prayed with her and I realised that a 'big' prayer would not be appropriate, but that she needed to know the love of Jesus in a very simple and direct way.

If we pray for someone in their own home as opposed to in a meeting we would almost certainly pray differently. In all of this we are asking how can we best help this person connect with God. The same applies even if the person is not a Christian. I love praying for those who do not profess an active faith in God because I know that, as they open themselves up to prayer, God will find a way of reaching into their lives. I often find that God gives us words of knowledge or insight in those situations simply to express His concern for them.

Perhaps praying for those who have been sick a long time is the hardest of all and, in a sensitive way, we need to help them to see that there are other possibilities apart from simply remaining sick. We also need to be honest with them and sometimes the best thing to do is to help prepare them for death, if the illness is terminal.

The more I pray for sick people the more I realise that there is a mind-set which seems to attack me. It goes something like this—it is difficult to get the sick healed! I have yet to find a Scripture to back it up and I realise how different it is from the mind of Christ! I have to attack that way of thinking constantly and allow God to renew my own mind.

When I come to pray for children, I find that many times God releases a greater depth of compassion in those situations, as it seems even more wrong that they should suffer. It is this compassion which is often the key to seeing a miracle taking place, and we all need to submit to God in greater depth so that we can begin to feel as He feels for those we pray with.

There are other situations which prove to be enormous battles, and we seldom break through on those until we have harnessed a number of people who will commit themselves to intercede and hear from God on those particular situations. Each situation is different, but God has answers for them all.

CHAPTER 5

HEALING AND WHOLENESS

God's will for our lives is pleasing and acceptable. In fact we could say that His will is exactly what we would choose if we were in receipt of all the facts. So we can state that the will of God is healing and not sickness. Sickness came as a result of the Fall and will be totally abolished in the age to come. There is no sickness in heaven, and we know that Jesus taught us to pray that the will of God might be done on earth in the same way as it is being done in heaven.

There are, however, a number of mistakes we can make on the subject of healing and the will of God. Firstly we can be so obsessed with physical health and well-being that we ignore some of the larger issues of life. We can so focus on physical healing that we forget that God is committed to wholeness. Also, we can fail to realise that God is working on the large canvas, whereas we tend to focus on that little bit which affects us and our lives. Having mentioned some of the dangers, however, I want to focus in this chapter on some of the areas which can stand in the way of God's healing.

God does heal supernaturally and His acts can transcend all natural laws, but on the subject of healing He also expects us to follow the natural laws of health, which also come from Him. This is how it was with Israel—they experienced the miraculous but He also gave them a set of natural health and dietary laws far more advanced than those of the surrounding nations.

If we are to experience God's wholeness, there are simple yet profound attitudes and approaches to life which we will need to follow. The Christian way of life is a healthy way of life because it touches us at every level—spiritual, emotional, relational and physical. The love which the Father shows to us is truly therapeutic and is the foundation for our experience of wholeness. Christianity brings a freedom from guilt and bitterness as well a high regard for the human body. Put these factors together and we have a very strong form of preventative medicine. If we are living our lives in harmony with God's word then we should be all the healthier in every aspect of our life as a result.

With that as a backdrop, we can look at some of the issues which often crop up when we get involved in praying for healing. These issues can, at times, become blockages to physical healing and we will certainly face some of them as we grow towards the wholeness which God wants to give. So the factors I list are not to be used as reasons why some don't get healed, but we will find at times that once some of the following issues have been dealt with, then healing results.

1. A faith problem

Many healing ministries home in on this problem. They teach that if a person is not healed then there is simply a lack of faith on the part of that person. It is true that Jesus often said that it was someone's faith that healed them, and it would be wrong of us to devalue the place of personal faith when it comes to seeking healing. However, this is not the only factor involved and I believe, if we are honest, the lack of faith is often with the person praying rather than with the person being prayed with. So I often find that a major blockage to healing is my lack of faith as the one praying, and I find it a continual challenge to allow God to increase my faith.

Another serious 'faith' problem is what I call *misbelief*. This is where a person is believing that God sends sickness to test and perfect us. When this is the case it is very difficult to bring a person to a place of receiving from God, because they are unconvinced that God would want to heal them.

The faith message, which has originated in the USA, has taught us very positively to continue to look to God for our health and to close the door to sickness. Some people need to hear this message more than others— particularly those who are always expecting to become sick. Whenever winter comes they expect to get the 'flu and normally their faith is rewarded! Such faith is dangerous as I believe it can open us up to sickness—and not always simply the 'flu. We need to guard our minds continually so that we are not allowing negative thoughts to dominate us. The power of positive thinking might not be a biblical doctrine, but it is certainly closer to the heart of Scripture than the power of negative thinking! Often, when counselling those who are sick, we will find that there is a door in this area which needs closing. It is particularly true where a disease has run in the family and a fatalistic expectation needs to be dealt with.

There is another side to the faith message which is less than positive. I occasionally find people who are so desperately trying to believe for their healing that they seem no longer to be expressing genuine faith in God, but to have a belief in a system. Our faith needs to be in God, not in a system. Ironically, faith in a method can become a blockage to healing, for with such an approach we can try so hard that God is effectively shut out.

One final factor that we can place under the general

heading of a faith problem is where there is insufficient trust being placed in the one giving the ministry. Faith must be in God for healing to be received, but Jesus also said that if His disciples were received then He Himself would be received (Matt. 10:40). It is important that when we pray with people they have a basic trust in us so that they can receive us with confidence. Where this is absent there can be a blockage to healing.

2. A receiving problem

Healing is a gift—and gifts must be both given and received. There are times when people have been badly damaged emotionally and have lived with such an overwhelming sense of rejection that they are unable to receive from God. They believe that God would do it for anyone else but not for them. In reality rejection is probably a far bigger problem than most of us are prepared to admit. Society often revolves around performance and at some point or other we all face areas where we do not reach the expected standard. If this is compounded by a difficult family background then there is often little basis on which to take a step of faith and to receive a free, unearned gift from God.

Jesus declared that His goal in salvation was to bring us to the Father. He said that He was the way which led to the Father (John 14:6). Knowing God as a Father was a major key in the life and ministry of Jesus and it is interesting to note that, on the occasions when God spoke from heaven over Jesus, it was to confirm His Sonship.[1] The Holy Spirit has been sent to confirm our sonship because it is from this relationship with God as our Father that our identity proceeds, as well as our sense of

---

1. The Father spoke from heaven over Jesus and underlined their relationship at His baptism and His transfiguration—see for example Mark 1:11; 9:7. He took time primarily to confirm Jesus relationally, not functionally.

self-worth and security. So rejection can block the reception of God's healing—it is a key area which God wants to touch in order to make us whole.

Usually strong prayer and counsel are needed to break the cycle of rejection in a person's life, and of course the church as the accepting community of God's people is the environment where this healing should take place. The gospel is the good news of God's acceptance of us regardless of race, social background or gender. He gives us value, regardless of any history of failure, and it is imperative that the church mirror His acceptance in dealing with people.

3. Guilt

The human personality is very complex. As medical science continues to advance, it is acknowledging more and more that internal feelings and emotions play a major factor in the external state of our health. In other words, our emotional state will have a bearing on our physical health. A major emotion is guilt and the human psychology is such that it finds it very difficult to live with guilt. The good news of the gospel is that Someone has dealt with our guilt. However, when the forgiveness of God is not received, there is really only one other way to deal with guilt and that is through punishment. At times it would seem that the human mind and emotions can produce illness in the physical realm as a means of punishment. If this is so then a certain amount of physical illness will be rooted in guilt.[2]

---

2. Gary Collins states that 'recent research has found that the physiological effects of self-blame accumulate over the years. If you blame yourself for a long enough period your body begins to deteriorate. Whenever tensions build in a person and are not released, the body weakens and eventually breaks down. Some psychiatrists view this as an unconscious form of punishment. Psychologically and emotionally it may be easier to tolerate pain than to bear the burden of guilt that would otherwise attract our attention' (Collins, Gary R., *Christian Counselling*, Nelson Word, 1989, page 141).

A similar line of argument is found in Betty Tapscott's book, *Set Free*, on pages 120–123 (Life Changing Books, 1978).

Real guilt should be easy to deal with in a Christian, in the sense that Christ died for us that we might be free. He did not carry some of the guilt and leave us to deal with the remainder—He carried it all. On the other hand, false guilt is harder to deal with. Christ did not carry false guilt and we will need to counsel people so that they are not weighed down with false guilt.

Much false guilt is rooted in childhood rejection. As a child grows up, its point of security is the adult world and it does not have the ability, nor the security, to challenge this adult world. If a child's parents do not show the love and care that it needs, then the child naturally assumes that there is something wrong with it, rather than that there are certain inadequacies in the parents. Such a child would grow up with the feeling 'there is something wrong with me'; this would then carry on through into adult life and result in an inordinate sense of false guilt and a corresponding over-inflated sense of responsibility.

Those who have been subjected to sexual abuse often carry this wrong sense of guilt and need careful, consistent counsel to lead them through to a place of freedom. Christ taught us to pray for the forgiveness of our debts to God as we forgive those who are our debtors. We owe God something, but it is also true that other people owe us something and at some point or other certain people will have let us down. In short, they are in debt to us. Forgiveness is taking the attitude that we do not want those people to pay for this: we release them debt-free. It is a choice we make and not an emotional feeling.

With those who suffer from false guilt, it is vital that we get them to face up to how they were let down, so that they can then follow through with an opportunity to forgive. Until they face up to where the blame lies they will never be free of this false sense of guilt.

4. Fear and anxiety

Fear is a very powerful emotion and we have all experienced its grip at times in our lives. David was a realist when he expressed that when he was afraid he put his trust in God. There were areas of his life where fear would grip him, but he knew in advance how he would respond in those situations (Ps. 56:3). The threat of illness is very real and at times fear can grip us in such a way that eventually the very thing we have feared is actually fulfilled (Job 3:25). This is why it is important that we do not give way to fear in our lives.

If the threat of illness looms large before us it is vital that we fill our mind with the positive concepts of God's love and care. John tells us that it is perfect love which drives out fear (1 John 4:18). Our English translations obscure the fact that John perceives this love coming to us through the body of believers. John maintains that God's love is made complete (same root Greek word as translated 'perfect' love) as we love one another (1 John 4:12). God has a community where He wants our fears to be dealt with—that community is the church. When we know the love of God through each other we will be in a place where we can confess our sins to one another, pray for one another and receive healing (Jas. 5:16).

Fear can be overcome as we actively replace the negative thought patterns with a positive trust in God and as we open up to one another, so discovering the healing power of God's accepting love. Anxiety and fear are tools the enemy uses to make us vulnerable to disease and problems. Faith and acceptance are God's answers.

5. Anger

Jesus became angry when He saw the devastation which the enemy had caused, so anger in itself is not a negative emotion when expressed against the work of the enemy.

There is, however, a negative side to anger and when this is expressed our bodies react with higher blood pressure, a release of adrenaline and a general tightness. Such anger does not promote wholeness but disease.

Alongside this expressed anger there is a type of unexpressed anger which is perhaps even more dangerous. Suppressed anger can be very dangerous simply because it has been locked up, with no means of expression. I believe such anger often finds its roots in rejection. Those who are quiet and reserved seem more prone to certain serious illnesses than those who are outspoken and this could well be because certain negative emotions, such as anger, have never been worked through.[3] So in counselling those who are sick we might find that anger—either expressed or unexpressed—needs to be faced and dealt with.

6. Bitterness

Perhaps bitterness and unforgiveness are the biggest hindrances to God bringing wholeness into us. We have already noted that Jesus taught us to pray that God will treat us in the same way as we treat those who wrong us (Matt. 6:12). Forgiveness from the heart was the only part of the prayer which Jesus subsequently picked up, to underline its importance in the verses which immediately follow the prayer outline (Matt. 6:14–15). In one of His parables Jesus taught that unforgiveness will cause us to end up in a prison where we will be tormented (Matt. 18:23–35). Because of Jesus' emphasis on the subject we need to note that there can be no real wholeness if forgiveness of others is not forthcoming, and many times

---

3. Personality types are often divided into Type A and Type B. Type A are more prone to having heart attacks but Type B are more prone to experiencing other diseases, including cancer. Although there probably needs to be more research on the subject, many in the medical profession would endorse this rather simplistic division.

even physical healing will be hindered from taking place.

7. Wrong relationships

God is not against friendship and relationship. In fact He invented companionship when He announced that a human being in isolation is 'not good' (Gen. 2:18). However, He knows that there are certain relationships which are unhelpful for us and some which are positively damaging. One relationship which is positively damaging is that of sexual experience which takes place outside marriage. It is not that God is anti-sex. It is simply that He is pro-marriage in a big way. He knows that sexual intercourse is more than simply a physical union and that a 'soul-tie' is normally formed in such cases. A transference of spirits can also take place, particularly if one of the parties has been involved with the occult.

There are other relationships which are non-sexual in nature which can cause problems. Even relationships with parents can become a factor which God wants to heal. This does not simply apply where the relationship is bad, but could occur where the relationship with parents is so close and claustrophobic that the person has not been allowed to grow up and is still living to please their parents. Unless this is dealt with gently but firmly the person will grow up somewhat stunted emotionally and if the problem is carried forward into marriage, then confusion and division will normally result.

Negative relationships are therefore another area where we will often need to target prayer if we are asking God to bring wholeness to someone.

8. Occult involvement or a curse

We cannot get involved with the work of the devil and expect that there will be no ramifications. Sometimes it would appear that people can receive healing through such practices as faith healing, but in every case there is a price to pay. The body might be healed, but there will be bondage in another area of the person's life. If someone has been involved with the occult this will normally need to be renounced and the person prayed with for freedom, even if the person has subsequently become a Christian.

Sometimes involvement with the occult seems to result in a curse taking effect over the individual's life which will need to be broken. However, curses can also take root through other means, and perhaps the most powerful are those which are self-imposed. I have discovered that many people have made a death-wish at some point in their life, which may result in a major depressive cycle taking effect. This can be in the form of wishing that they had never been born, or wishing that they had been born a girl if they are male and vice versa. This is a form of death-wish, because if this is my experience I am really saying that if I could disappear and another person come in my place, then I would be content.

Sometimes this downward death cycle can take root because of serious grief that has been experienced in the family. Another similar situation can exist when there has been a miscarriage. If the effects are particularly traumatic some of the subsequent children can be born with this grief/death-wish on them. I suppose the reason for this is that it can be very hard to work through the grieving process in those circumstances. In the case of the death of someone who has been born there is a person with whom we have had a relationship to grieve over, but in the case of the unborn child the loss has not been with a person with whom the mother and others have had a relationship. The loss is real, but the grieving process can be more difficult.

With regard to physical illness I believe it is very

important that we do not end up hating our own bodies. This is perhaps more pertinent for women, who seem to be endlessly subjected to images of what the perfect female body should look like, than for men. We are not to be paranoid about every negative thought we have ever had about ourselves or our bodies, but we need to realise that where the feeling has been particularly strong or persistent, there will almost certainly be physical or emotional problems as a result. Repentance and prayer will be required in those situations.

9. Hereditary roots

A number of physical difficulties are the result of a natural genetic situation, but some are caused by spirits which have been able to enter the family line. Spirit problems will often be the result of occult involvement or serious sexual misconduct in previous generations. These situations will obviously need prayer for freedom and any physical problem will not normally be healed until the spiritual roots have been dealt with.

10. Self-pity

Self-pity is a powerful emotion and one to which we are all tempted to succumb. At times Jesus asked people a very direct question along the lines of 'Do you want to get well?' I think He asked this because for some of the people He dealt with this was a very real issue. If He were to heal them they would have to face life head on, and would no longer be able to use their illness to obtain sympathy and an easier way of life. If we sense this might be the situation with someone, we need to approach it with great care and compassion, because many sick people need real affection and the last thing they need is to be told that they don't really want to get better. However, at times, this is an issue which we cannot avoid and need to tackle with great wisdom.

11. Lack of persistence

We all like instant answers to our problems, but I am convinced there are some who are not healed simply because they do not persist and continue to ask for prayer. I have noticed through my travels in Africa that people there tend to have an attitude to prayer for healing very different from ours. In England, if a person has been prayed for and has not been healed, that experience becomes a negative factor and often discourages them from opening themselves up to further prayer for healing. They have tried healing and it did not work! In Africa a person who has received prayer for healing but does not on that occasion receive healing will come back again and again. The mentality is that it is not possible to receive the laying on of hands this many times and not be healed—it must work one of these times! I think I know which approach is healthier.

I often remark that if we approached the medical profession with the same lack of persistence we would drive them mad. If our doctor prescribes treatment which does not work we return, asking for some further treatment. We tend to persevere until we find a cure. I would love to see Christians in the UK take that same approach when they ask God for healing. I am sure the number of testimonies of healing would rise dramatically.

12. Wrong lifestyle

Some healing may depend on a change to the person's lifestyle. We cannot continue to live lives of great stress and then expect to be disease-free. It is often good to examine our lives and ask how well we are pacing ourselves. We do not want to burn out for Jesus, but to burn on for Him. Hard work is part of the Christian ethos, but so is rest. The same God who said 'work six days' also said 'rest one in seven'.

The above is not an exhaustive list of all the issues at stake in healing and wholeness, but I hope it illustrates that physical healing is often much more than simply a physical problem. When someone comes for physical healing we will need to discern where the root of the problem lies. We will need to receive wisdom from God to understand what He is seeking to do at this time in this person's life. Through all this, it is important that we do not try to operate by rules—God does not live by a rule book but by His holiness and love.

Sometimes at the root of the sickness is a demonic problem. Jesus discerned this in the case of the woman who was bound in her back with a crippling disease (Luke 13:16). Evil spirits can be discerned through the gift of discernment of spirits, or they can be discovered (sometimes much to our surprise!). We might discover them as we talk and realise that there has been a long history of occult involvement or something similar. If we discover or discern the presence of evil spirits, we need not only to set the person free but to close the doors of entry to the problem.

The doors of entry might have been voluntary, and if so, it is important that the person closes the door through renunciation and repentance. The doors might have been hereditary and it is then important that we cut them free from their family history. Other times the doors have been opened through a trauma which will often require emotional healing as well as deliverance. Sometimes the entry point is where the person has been sinned against (for example, sexual abuse) and bringing freedom from guilt and ensuring there has been forgiveness will be necessary to bring total freedom to that person. Even after the ministry there might still need to be some significant changes of lifestyle.

When we pray against the presence of evil spirits, it is important that we pray with conviction and not in a half-hearted way. As we begin to pray we will find a resistance, and then the resistance will suddenly lift when the problem has been effectively dealt with.

In summary

It is important that as we come to minister to people we do not assume there are a host of problems to be overcome. If we fall into that trap we will not be surprised when the person is not healed, and eventually will never be in faith for healing. This is not a good basis on which to pray for sick people! We need to get on, love the person and pray for them with confidence.

It is best not to focus on the problems but the answer. This is true both for the person praying and for the person being prayed with. As we focus on Jesus, His love and provision we will find that many of the problems disappear and that Jesus releases His healing power. He loves to bring us into wholeness and it is a privilege to be involved with Him in this process, so we need to treat people with the same dignity and care that He does. It is His love and care which are so vital if true healing and wholeness are to be found.

CHAPTER 6

RELEASING THE SUPERNATURAL

Christianity is fundamentally supernatural. A faith which maintains that we can have an intimate relationship with the God who oversees the entire universe can only be described as supernatural. The supernatural can invade our whole life, but the mistake we should not make is to assume that the supernatural is always spectacular.

The writer of the book of Hebrews affirms that the powers of the age to come are already here and that believers have tasted of these powers (Heb. 6:5). The age to come is continually breaking in on this age and disturbing the status quo. God loves to overrule where Satan has been ruling: He loves to undo and outdo whatever Satan has done. Furthermore, He loves to do this through ordinary people. I have been very taken with Luke's account of Saul of Tarsus' conversion. Jesus intervenes directly in the situation and in no uncertain terms confronts him and his behaviour. That part of the story I find believable—the part I find so difficult to believe is that Jesus then stops the conversation and leaves the directive word about Saul's future in the hands of a disciple called Ananias (Acts 9:1–19). If I had been the Lord I would not have entrusted such a key element to anyone—certainly not to someone who is simply described as a disciple. If I had had to use someone it would have been a well-known apostle. The account highlights how God wants to use the ordinary person in extraordinary ways. The supernatural is for all of us.

I want to devote this chapter to some perspectives on releasing the supernatural power of God's Spirit. The supernatural is not always a comfortable realm and we will feel at times that we are right on the edge. This is not a bad feeling because we need to realise that if God does not show up then we certainly can't take over and produce the goods. If we have not already discovered this, we will soon find out that we cannot dictate to God how and when He moves supernaturally. We are here to serve Him, and not vice versa.

If we are going to move in the supernatural there are certain key elements which it will be essential for us to have in place. Some of these are for our own safety and well-being, while others will help keep us in touch with a God who is supernatural.

Discover God's Father-heart

Jesus' key to His own ministry and life is found in His relationship with His Father. He simply came to do His Father's will and spoke the words He heard His Father speak. He made everything so simple and set for us the true model for ministry. He taught His disciples to pray from this basis, telling them not to fret about their needs because they were coming to a Father who understood all their needs even before they presented them to Him. They were not to fall into the trap of thinking that God would hear them if they prayed for a long period of time, but to come and begin by acknowledging the dynamic relationship they were now experiencing (Matt. 6:5–15). In His own inimitable way Jesus cut right across so much of the religious nonsense we can all get involved in. Most of us still fall into the trap of feeling that if we prayed more then God would do more for us. While there is truth in this, Jesus did not concentrate on the *amount* of prayer but the *relationship* which is expressed as we pray. The more we know God as Father, the more we will find God answering our prayers.

If we know God as Father then we will be in a good place to be able to handle both success and failure. Success will not go to our head, because our security will not be found in how well we perform, and conversely failure will not paralyse us. I have found with many people—including some significant ministries—that they are totally dependent on how well they perform, and this is a very dangerous base from which to minister.

I have read about the ministries of many of those who moved in healing in the USA between 1948 and 1958 in what has been called the Healing Revival, and have been very impressed by their passion for God and the release of power that they experienced.[1] However, I have also noticed that many of them seem to have been driven by a need to succeed. It seems to me that many of them lived with great insecurity and as a result, in later life, some of them lost their relationship with God. In looking at their upbringings I have noticed that many of them grew up with a deep sense of rejection and isolation. Many of them had tragic backgrounds and perhaps this drove them to seek God for power and significance. However, the power of God is no substitute for knowing His love. Only love can heal the rejection syndrome, and it is for this reason I place the need to know the Father-heart of God as the top priority for anyone who wishes to move in the supernatural. The Holy Spirit has come not only to

1. This move is documented very favourably and accurately in *All Things are Possible* by David Edwin Harrell, Jr. (Indiana University Press, 1975).

heal and to release power but primarily to cause us to cry out 'Abba, Father' (Rom. 8:15; Gal. 4:6).

If we fail to know God as Father we will be a danger to ourselves, as the enemy will be able to pick us off fairly easily. We will also be a danger to others as those who are on a performance trip often project onto others their own insecurities. If we know God as Father then we will be sufficiently secure to get involved in situations, and we will also be secure in saying 'no' to other situations. We will be delighted with our successes, but our failures will not devastate us.

Know the Holy Spirit

The manifestations or gifts flow from and through Him, therefore we will need to learn how to submit to Him and His leadings. If we are to move in the supernatural we will need to become sensitive to Him. This sensitivity is not simply learning to hear Him for words of knowledge or the like, but learning to hear Him when He speaks to us about ourselves. We will need to be quick to respond when He challenges us about our own life or motives.

One of the most tragic stories in the Bible is of Samson, who did not know that the Lord had left him (Judg. 16:20). The coming of the Spirit can be dramatic, but when His anointing lifts we are often unaware of it. So we will need to cultivate our fellowship with the Holy Spirit, to know His leadings and that still small inner voice.

There is much debate over the rights and wrongs of praying to the Holy Spirit but we must come to the place where we know Him and are unafraid to have fellowship with Him. Personally I am happy, in certain situations, to pray to the Holy Spirit but, even if that is an uncomfortable position for us to take, I believe we need at least to learn how to talk with Him as a friend.

Follow hard after Jesus

Jesus must become our primary role model, for He said that we will do the works that He did and even greater (John 14:12). It is important that we seek to emulate Him, not simply in the works but in how He did those works. I occasionally consider the ministries of some of those who move in the supernatural, and admire the signs and wonders, but ask myself, 'Would Jesus do it that way?' However, I find that I cannot simply leave it there, but have to ask myself whether Jesus would do it my way. It might not be a comfortable question but we must insist that Jesus needs to be our role model.

I am constantly amazed at the stories of healing surrounding the ministry of Jesus. I marvel at the way He met people at their point of need and dealt with them in exactly the right way. He did not operate from a set of principles, but was always people-focused. Anyone who aspires to move in healing needs to read over and over the Gospel records of Jesus—they are so informative and challenging.

If we focus on Jesus we will get a picture of His victory which will inspire us and build faith. We will also see how He treated everyone with respect, which will inspire us to love people more. Beyond that we will see His normality, as well as the supernatural dimension which surrounded His life.

Prayer and fasting (Matt. 6:5–18)

There is a price to pay for moving in the supernatural. On

one occasion when the disciples had met with failure, Jesus told them the reason was that there had been insufficient prayer on their part (Mark 9:29). Prayer is not a work which earns us merit marks with God, but Jesus was clear that, when we pray with the right motivation and from the right relationship, there is a reward He wants to give us. The same is true for fasting, which seems to be simply another form of praying. Fasting is a prophetic act which declares we are not prepared to live simply by physical bread, but need the word of God to be our sustenance (Matt. 4:4—in the context of Jesus' fast).

I am convinced that Jesus wants us in constant communion with Him, which must be the continual prayer that Paul speaks of in 1 Thessalonians 5:17. Alongside this there are seasons when God will lead us to seek Him in a far more intense way, and they will result in a greater breakthrough in the supernatural. This seems to be the pattern which Jesus followed. He was in constant contact with His Father, but also had specific times of intense prayer particularly before key events in His life.

Fasting does play a part, but it is not a question of how much we fast but of responding to God when He speaks. Fasting demonstrates that the material things of this world are not as important to us as God's power and presence. Fasting is a wonderful way of disciplining our fleshly appetites and helping to attune us to God in new ways. On a practical note, it is best to set attainable goals rather than end up feeling condemned when we fail to achieve goals which prove unrealistic.

Exercise spiritual gifts

Spiritual gifts are not simply for Christian gatherings. We

need to exercise them outside meetings and in life. If we have the opportunity to walk out and enjoy creation, we can prophesy the will of God over creation. We can take the opportunity to prophesy the coming of God's kingdom into situations (or perhaps this is simply what prayer should be, for Jesus said, 'When you pray, say . . . '—Luke 11:2).

Speaking in tongues is a very powerful gift, for through it we edify ourselves (1 Cor. 14:4). It is good to speak in tongues in the course of life, for by so doing we will exercise our spirits in a unique way. Healing and tongues are both manifestations of the Holy Spirit (1 Cor. 12:7) and so as we move in one we will find it easier to move in the other.

Learn obedience over the small things

Many times in order to see a move of the supernatural we will need to move out in obedience to God. In the ministry of Jesus we see that He occasionally acted in a strange way in order to perform a miracle. We can only presume that He put mud on the blind man's eyes out of obedience to God's word to Him, and there will be times when God will tell us to do something which demonstrates our trust in Him in order to see a miracle. There have been occasions when I have felt God say to me to hit a person in the area of their sickness, as I have prayed with them. That is never a comfortable thing to do, but we need to learn obedience in these things. If we are to learn to hear the voice of God accurately then we will need to learn obedience over the small things in life.

If we desire to have words of knowledge then we will also need to be ready to respond to God about simply encouraging someone else. We learn to hear God through those small things. In one sense there is not much at stake—except our obedience. We cannot simply sit around saying we will wait for God to speak a big word to us and then we will obey, if we are not prepared to step out on the small things He speaks to us.

Discipline our speech

If we want God to endorse our words when we pray for the sick, we also need to realise that God does not adopt a sacred/secular approach to life. He does not want to come and endorse our words only when we are in spiritual mode, but not when we are outside the context of a meeting. So we will need to discipline our speech so that we are not expressing destruction and hatred in one sphere but seeking to speak words of release and healing in another. In the words of James, 'This should not be' (Jas. 3:10). If we want God to back up our words then perhaps we should examine what words we tend to speak when we are outside the 'spiritual' context.

Boldness is a key (Acts 4:29–30; 14:3)

There are very few prayers recorded in Scripture which give us a clue about how the early church prayed in relation to the supernatural, but we do find one in Acts chapter 4. In the face of great opposition they simply request that God will give them great boldness for they have a conviction that God Himself will then move with power. Boldness is not arrogance but it is vital if we are to see God move. True boldness will be against the works of darkness and expressed positively in relation to our proclamation of the truths which centre in Christ.

Perseverance (Heb. 10:35, 36)

Nothing comes automatically—there are no free lunches. If nothing happens automatically we will need to push through with our quest to see God move supernaturally through us. We will need to keep the vision in focus and seek to play our part in moving towards that goal.

On the one hand I am desperate to see God move with great power, but on the other hand all I want to know is that I have played my part towards that end. Even if we do not see all we would like to see in our own lifetime, or through our own ministry or church, it is important that we have played our part in our generation and have the satisfaction of knowing that we have at least passed on the baton to someone else, or to another generation. God wants us to be faithful and so we will need to exercise perseverance in our approach to healing and the supernatural.

There is more to life than the supernatural, but God loves to give us the experience of seeing the powers of the age to come breaking through into this age and, if we are to be effective instruments for Him, I believe the areas outlined in this chapter will be important. In the next chapter I want to look at the whole area of moving in revelation and the anointing of the Spirit as we bring this study to a close.

CHAPTER 7

THE HOLY SPIRIT AND HEALING

The Holy Spirit has come to bring us into a living relationship with God as our Father and also to enable us to fulfil the call of God on our lives. There are two very important areas of His work which we will need to know if we are going to be effective in healing. The first is His anointing and the second is the revelation which He can bring to us.

The Holy Spirit and His anointing

The anointing of the Holy Spirit is very difficult to define, but it is evident when present and even more evident when absent! The anointing of the Holy Spirit enables us to perform the tasks God asks us to do with ease. In short, when the anointing of the Holy Spirit is in evidence, things happen.

There are many different anointings of the Spirit, but I want to focus on the anointing which God sends on us or on a gathering of His people at a particular time. This is not to say that this is the only anointing or the most important, but it is certainly a key factor when seeking to move in healing in a corporate setting.

We need to flow with the anointing that God gives and in order to do that we must ask two basic questions—where is the anointing, and what has God sent His anointing to perform? The answers to those questions will determine how we respond and how well we flow with the anointing of the Spirit.

God can send His Spirit with power upon us as an individual and, if this is the case, we need to move forward with confidence and release what God has placed upon us. This will normally be accompanied by a sense of confidence and boldness. He can equally release an anointing on the corporate gathering and, if this is so, we need, in the light of that, to seek to help them to release their faith in God. If the anointing of the Spirit has come because of a message which has been spoken we would do well to move forward trying to draw out the points which the Holy Spirit has highlighted during the message.

As well as knowing where the anointing is, we need to determine what the anointing has been sent to do. If we fail here we might well end up very frustrated as we try to work against the Holy Spirit. Some examples of the different reasons why God has sent a tangible anointing might be: to release a flow of prophecy and revelation, or to bring emotional or physical healing. A key factor then is to discern why the Holy Spirit has come. We might be desiring to see a move of physical healing, but if God is doing a work of emotional healing we will be far more effective if we simply flow with Him and leave our desires on one side.

Having discerned the anointing of the Holy Spirit, we then need to find a starting point and it is important that we do not rush in, but decide where or with whom we should start. We can ask God to give us eyes to see with whom He is at work, or, failing that, we can make a start in an area where we have faith.

The anointing of the Spirit can be very powerful and

when it comes in that way we need to step out with boldness and move with the Spirit. At such times it is best not to get into long conversations with people but to pray with confidence, knowing that the Name of Jesus is higher than every other name on the face of this earth. When a dimension of power of that order is released it is not at all uncommon for many people to be 'slain in the Spirit', but it is important that we do not look for outward manifestations, making an outward sign our goal. Our goal must continue to be helping people to connect with God.

The Holy Spirit and revelation

The Holy Spirit often gives revelation to us when we pray for people. This may come in the form of words of knowledge and we may discover that God is showing us certain things in this person's life which He now wants to deal with. Such 'words' can come in a variety of ways and sometimes they can take us quite by surprise. When we first begin to step out with such words we will probably need some help and advice as to how to discern the voice of God, but I find that when God gives me a word, faith also comes with it. By that I do not mean that all doubt also disappears, because it is very possible (and probably normal) for doubt and faith to reside in us at the same time. Our task is to believe God and to doubt our doubts.

I have also found that a major barrier I must overcome is the desire not to look foolish, but we must make a quality decision to honour Jesus regardless of how we look in the process. If we make that decision we will have the great thrill of knowing that He is pleased with us.

When God gives us revelation we have to decide

what we are going to do with it and we will need wisdom in deciding how to handle it. Often we should share what God gives us even if it does not all make sense to us. I remember one time stating that there was someone present whom God had wanted to heal. The event had occurred in November of 1977 and that November was a cold month! I can remember people looking at me a little strangely, and understandably so. At the close of the meeting someone came forward to explain how in that month she had moved, amidst trauma, from the southern hemisphere to the northern. For her, November 1977 was a cold month. I may have looked a little foolish, but that person knew how much God loved her.

There are other times when we can actually abuse the words which God gives us by so intimidating people that they end up feeling we know everything about them. I believe that is an abuse and we need to find ways of exposing them to God's knowledge and love, not ours. In those cases I find it far better simply to pray, thanking God that He knows everything about them and then try to include some of the things that He knows—almost from the position of a bystander. This normally has the effect of opening them to God, so that they almost fail to notice that we are there.

God loves to help us, but there are certain pitfalls we need to avoid. We should seek to avoid being drawn in simply through sympathy, or where there is such a strong desire from others that we are manipulated into going beyond what God has given to us. We should move at the pace with which we are comfortable, avoiding the pressure of making things happen. One final word of advice—don't look too hard at people's faces, as they can be an intimidating factor!

With regard to words of knowledge, we also need to teach people that it is not necessary for someone to give a word which describes their situation in order for them to be healed. I am convinced that certain people are asking for a word of knowledge concerning their situation, rather than asking God for the solution. If we are sick we need healing, not a word of knowledge, although many times the healing will come through the word of knowledge.

Losing the anointing

If we are not careful we can very easily lose the anointing which God gives us. We can lose the anointing through sin and disobedience. We can also 'dry up' if we continually give out more that we take in and so lose the anointing of God. A third way of losing the anointing is far more subtle, but equally damaging. We can lose God's anointing through discouragement. I owe the above thoughts to Dudley Daniel, who points out that we could find God using people who are evidently in sin, but that we will find very few discouraged men and women whom God is using powerfully.

We do need to guard against sin, but sometimes we are unaware that the enemy might simply be seeking to wear us down through discouragement. I trust that this small book will be an encouragement to many to step out and not give up. We need to keep on keeping on. Healing has been in great evidence in the past, and certainly will be again in the future, but our privilege and commission is to taste today of the powers that are to come.

NEW TESTAMENT EXCEPTIONS

Paul and his thorn in the flesh (2 Cor. 12:1–10)

This passage of Scripture is often quoted to show that Paul suffered from sickness, and therefore we too should expect to suffer in the same way. However, we need to establish exactly what Paul was referring to here before we draw the above conclusion. Paul helps us here in a number of ways—firstly he describes this thorn as a messenger (Greek word *angelos:* angel or messenger) from Satan. He is very clear that the source of his problem was Satan and not God, although even in that he could clearly see that God was using it for His glory.

This messenger 'continually pounded' Paul (NIV: 'torment'; the Greek verb is *kolaphizo*, from the noun meaning 'a fist', and Paul uses the continual tense here, hence my translation as above). So Paul experienced a continual pounding from the enemy in a certain sphere of his life and it would seem that the problems he faced, which he lists for us in verse 10, are very likely to be the outworking of this messenger's work—'I delight in weaknesses, in insults, in hardships, in persecutions, in difficulties.'

He also describes this messenger as 'a thorn in my flesh'. This was not at all an uncommon term for those who were enemies of God's people. In Numbers 33:55

Israel's neighbours are described as potential thorns in their sides (see also Joshua 23:13, Judges 2:3 and Ezekiel 28:24). If we take all this together we are presented with a situation where Paul is continually harassed or pounded by enemies of God. The most likely scenario is that he is referring to the 'Judaisers' who seemed to follow him around and correct his theology, by telling his converts that they needed to obey all the law of Moses if they were to be proper Christians. We cannot be certain, but this would seem to fit with the context much better than the idea that he is referring to a sickness at this point. It is, incidentally, the viewpoint of Chrysostum (347–407) who suggested that the leader of this group of Judaisers was the thorn. This viewpoint was followed by two other 'church fathers', Hilary and Augustine.

If it were a sickness we know that he asked God to remove it, until he heard very clearly God's response. In other words he took the biblical approach to sickness, which is to resist it. Paul's account of the answer God gave him is very revealing. He used a Greek perfect tense when he said 'he said to me', which means that the answer was still as fresh as it was on the day that God spoke. God's word was still alive for him and he now lived with the fact that God's power was manifested whenever he was weak. He was not looking for outward strength and for his circumstances to be ideal, but for God to be manifested in power wherever he went. He described this in 1 Corinthians 2:3–4 when he said, 'I came to you in weakness and fear, and with much trembling. My message and my preaching were not with wise and persuasive words, but with a demonstration of the Spirit's power.'

Paul and his illness in Galatia (Gal. 4:12–16)

The New International Version leaves us in no doubt that
Paul suffered from an illness when he came to Galatia the
first time (see 4:13). However this translation is not the
only nor indeed the most likely possibility. The Greek
word for 'sickness' (*astheneia*) is also translated as
'weakness' and we can decide how best to translate it
from the context. Paul further helps us here by defining
the type of weakness which he experienced—he says it
was a weakness of the flesh (*astheneia tes sarkes*). The only
other time this phrase occurs in the New Testament is
also in one of Paul's letters, in Romans 6:19, where the NIV
translates the phrase as 'weak in your natural selves'. So
the NIV understands the phrase there as simply meaning
human weakness as opposed to divine strength.

Paul also says that this occurred in his first visit to
Galatia (the Greek here is *to proteron*: 'the first time') so by
going back to the book of Acts we can discover exactly
what he is referring to. Paul first came to the province of
Galatia in Acts 14:6, where the Lycaonian cities
mentioned were part of the Roman province of Galatia.
The reason why he preached there was because of a plot
by both Jews and Gentiles to kill him and Barnabas, and
so they fled to the cities of Lystra and Derbe in fear of
their lives. He preached for the first time in Galatia, not
because of a direct word from the Lord, but because of 'a
weakness in his flesh'. In other words he was probably
terrified! We need to get rid of the idea that Paul never
had fears (see 1 Cor. 2:3–4). The difference between Paul
and ourselves is that in spite of his fears he got on with
his commission of preaching the gospel, for then he knew
that God would show up with power.

The reference to the people taking out their eyes and
giving them to Paul (Gal. 4:15) has been used to

substantiate the theory that he was ill and suffered from severe eye problems. However, it seems better to take this to be a simple overstatement to describe their enthusiastic response to him and his message. If he had meant to stress that this was a literal thing they wanted to do, he would have been more likely to reverse the word order in the Greek and place the word 'your' at the beginning of the phrase (he uses the order *tous ophthalmous humon* and not *humon tous ophthalmous*). So, in conclusion, the historical reference does not make it seem likely that this was a reference to a physical sickness. (If Paul had qualified this weakness as a weakness of the *body* we would have to draw a different conclusion from the one above.)

Paul and eye problems

There are passages other than the one above which are cited to support the theory that Paul had a serious eye problem. When put together they can present a credible picture, but when examined individually they are far from convincing.

Galatians 6:11 is used to back this view because Paul says, 'See what large letters I use as I write to you with my own hand!' The argument goes that Paul wrote in large letters because he suffered from an eye disease. However, the most likely scenario is that Paul is contrasting his own writing style with that of a professional amanuensis (or secretary). Paul normally dictated his letters and occasionally signed them off himself (see 1 Cor. 16:21 or 2 Thess. 3:17), but with this letter it appears he wrote it all himself. (He uses a Greek past tense here, not the present tense as in the above two references.) By drawing their attention to this he is emphasising his great love and commitment to them.

Another reference used to support the theory is Acts 23:1–5, where Paul insults the high priest and then defends himself by explaining that he did not realise that this person was the high priest. This could have been because he could not see him due to his severe eye problem, but a more likely explanation is that this was not a regular session of the Sanhedrin (Acts 22:30 tells us it was called by the commander) and so the high priest was probably not wearing his distinctive robes, nor would he have occupied his usual place. In addition, Paul's visits to Jerusalem over the past twenty years or more had been infrequent and so he would almost certainly not have known Ananias by sight.

Other situations

Timothy was told to take a little wine for his stomach's sake (1 Tim. 5:23). Here Paul gives a very practical solution to a problem Timothy was experiencing with the polluted water at Ephesus. God is practical and some-times not as spiritual as we are!

There might have been another contributing factor in the mix which meant that Timothy was more susceptible than others to stomach problems. When Paul writes to Timothy he has to continue to remind him not to be fear-ful, and it seems that Timothy had a particular difficulty in this area. Often those who are affected by fear find that one of the results is that they live with a 'weak' stomach. Perhaps we could also infer that Timothy had never been properly 'fathered' by the lack of specific reference to his father, in contrast to the prominence that both his mother and grandmother have in his life. Again, often those who have never been fathered adequately have fear in their lives—but this is perhaps to read too much into the passages referring to Timothy and his family.

Epaphroditus was someone who became extremely ill and indeed almost died (Phil. 2:25–30). However, it appears clear that God intervened in his situation, for Paul says that God had mercy on him. In verse 30 Paul gives us some insight into the background to the circumstances surrounding Epaphroditus' illness. He states that he had risked his life in the work of the gospel. Paul uses the Greek verb *paraballo*, which was a gambling term used of throwing down dice, and it seems that Epaphroditus was prepared even to throw his own life down for the sake of the gospel. This needs to be a warning to us not to 'gamble' with our lives even if we do so for the sake of the gospel. We cannot do the work of the Holy Spirit for Him. We need to live with the tension of working hard for the gospel's sake, but also learning to relax and allowing God to do what only He can do.

Finally we read of Trophimus whom Paul left ill at Miletus (2 Tim. 4:20). There is little surrounding evidence to this story and we can only accept it at face value without any real comment. We do not know whether Trophimus experienced a process of healing or not.

Conclusion

We can use these possible exceptions to healing in the New Testament either as a reason why God will not heal, or as an encouragement to press on. Even if these are clear situations where God did not break in and heal we must resist the temptation to build on the exceptions rather than the clear teaching of Scripture.

I'M NOT HEALED—
WHAT NOW?

One of the most discouraging situations we can find ourselves in is to have been prayed with on a number of different occasions, and yet find that we have not been healed. Each time that prayer does not result in healing it only seems to underline that God is not going to do it for us.

I believe we need to deal with the discouragement side of the problem first of all. Being sick is not a sin—nor is it an indication that God is displeased with us if we are not healed. The enemy often uses the situation I describe to attack us where we are most vulnerable—it either makes us feel guilty (the 'I-don't-have-enough-faith' syndrome) or we withdraw from God because we begin to question our relationship with Him. So we need to take this ground from the enemy and make a declaration that God is committed to us and this sickness has got nothing to do with God finding me unacceptable. If we experience nothing else through the situation, other than the fact that God loves us unconditionally, then we have come a long way.

If we do not nail these issues we will continually be looking for a reason why we are sick or have not been healed. If God speaks a specific word then we do need to respond, but the problem with self-examination of this sort is that there is often no answer.

Having made a good start, where should we go from here? Firstly, let me underline that there is nothing wrong with seeking medical advice and help alongside pursuing prayer. This only becomes an issue of faith if God has specifically spoken in our situation that to pursue medical advice would be a wrong course.

However, assuming that we want to look to God to heal it is important that we begin to build our faith in God's healing ability and desire. This is not because there is a certain amount of faith which is needed—we don't want to get trapped into trying to answer the unanswerable question of 'How much is enough?' But as we begin to build our faith we will move ourselves towards the place where we are ready to receive from God. How do we do this? We need to understand that faith only comes through hearing God for ourselves. This means that we will need to expose ourselves to those who are ministering in a faith-filled way—either through preaching, lifestyle, books or tapes.

As we hear truth about God, His character and His desire to heal, our inner picture of ourselves and our situation will begin to change. We will begin to lose the image that this problem is permanent and begin to see that when Jesus comes He approaches these situations as if the problem was merely temporary (or subject to change).

By doing this we will be placing ourselves in a great position to receive prayer. Our attitude will begin to change and we will increasingly feel that if we were not healed last time, then it is more likely (rather than less likely) next time. This is considerably better than the approach that says 'I've been prayed for (once) and it didn't work!'

A final word of encouragement: I have found that my faith has grown the most when God has not healed me instantly, but when I have continued to believe in God's love for me and then finally He has come and healed me, even though as time went on it had seemed less and less likely (to the natural mind) that God would in fact do this.

So what do we do when we face this situation? Don't give up. We need to be secure in the knowledge that we are loved by God—but give healing a go. As we open ourselves to God, His love and His word, we will have nothing to lose—other than the sickness.

RECOMMENDED READING

There are many good books on the subject of healing and I can only mention a few here. Those I list below I have found helpful. I do not necessarily endorse the contents any more than I would expect the authors of those books to endorse the contents of this book, but I suggest to anyone who is interested in healing that they read widely rather than limit themselves to authors with whom they agree. There are diverse viewpoints but I have gained enormously from being exposed to a variety of approaches.

Andrews, Ian, *Building a People of Power* (Nelson Word, 1988)

Blue, Ken, *The Authority to Heal* (Monarch, 1989)

Bosworth, F. F., *Christ the Healer* (Fleming H. Revell, 1973)

Copeland, Gloria, *And Jesus Healed Them All* (KCP Publications, 1984)

Cornwall, Judson, *Unfeigned Faith* (Kingsway, 1985)

Glennon, Jim, *Your Healing is Within You* (Hodder & Stoughton, 1979)

——, *How Can I Find Healing?* (Hodder & Stoughton, 1984)

MacNutt, Francis, *The Prayer that Heals* (Hodder & Stoughton, 1983)

——, *The Power to Heal* (Ave Maria Press, 1977)

——, *Healing* (Hodder & Stoughton, 1989)

Marshall, Tom, *Healing from the Inside Out* (originally published under the title *Foundations for a Healing Ministry*, Sovereign World, 1988)

McMillan, S. I., *None of These Diseases* (Marshall Pickering, 1989)

Pfeifer, Samuel, *Healing at Any Price* (Nelson Word, 1988)

Prince, Derek, *Faith to Live By* (Kingsway, 1984)

Sipley, Richard, *Understanding Divine Healing* (Scripture Press Foundations, 1986)

Urquhart, Colin, *Receive Your Healing* (Hodder & Stoughton, 1986)

Wimber, John, and Springer, Kevin, *Power Evangelism* (Hodder & Stoughton, 1985)

——, *Power Healing* (Hodder & Stoughton, 1986)